Civil Servants,
Ministers and Parliament

Civil Servants, Ministers and Parliament

Martin Stanley

This edition published in Great Britain in 2024 by
Richborne Publishing
68 Richborne Terrace
London
SW8 1AX
Copyright © Martin Stanley 2024

978-1-7392764-3-0

A CIP catalogue record for this book is available from the British Library.

Set in 11.75pt / 17.6pt Baskerville Regular

Produced in Great Britain by
Bluemoon Design Studio, Bristol, BS2 0BY

www.civilservant.org.uk

MIX
Paper from
responsible sources
FSC® C114687
FSC
www.fsc.org

Contents

This book describes and discusses the constitutional and ethical framework which governs the behaviour of UK civil servants.

The first four chapters summarise the UK's constitution and list all the main ethical rules with which civil servants must comply. These are collectively often referred to as the Westminster Model of Government[1].

This description of civil servants' duties is supplemented by comment and practical advice from experienced officials. This includes, for instance, guidance on how to maintain political impartiality, and what civil servants should do (if anything) if Ministers do not take their advice, or if Ministers appear to be 'behaving badly'.

---

[1] This phrase is useful for many purposes but it has no precise or widely agreed definition.

Chapters five and six focus on the many pressures on, and criticisms of, the Westminster Model and describe how civil servants may, as a result, be becoming increasingly accountable to Parliament.

Chapter 1

1.1 Introduction

The culture of the civil service is quite unlike that of any other organisation in the UK. Civil servants are expected to be highly professional 'serial monogamists':- intensely loyal to their current Ministers but ready to switch allegiance whenever there is a change of government. They are simultaneously expected to respect the vital role of Parliament.

This relationship between civil servants, Ministers and Parliament was admired, and emulated to a greater or lesser extent, in many other countries. It still has its admirers but it also nowadays has many critics who argue that it is outdated and not fit for the modern world. The first three chapters of this book accordingly describe the culture and ethics of the civil service as summarised in the Civil Service Code and elsewhere. The remainder of the book discusses what seems to be going wrong, and what might be done about it.

To set the scene, this extract from a 1949 *Handbook for the New Civil Servant* very nicely summarises the way in which the working methods of all civil servants - not just those in Whitehall - were designed so as to facilitate impartiality and accountability to Parliament.

> The first thing that strikes many people, when they come into a Government office for the first time, is the importance that the Civil Service attaches to papers - files, memoranda, written records of all kinds. A good deal of the work of the Civil Service, of course, is done by telephone or by personal conversation, but you will find that anything important or new has to be recorded on paper somewhere, sooner or later; and in all probability a large part of your work will consist of dealing with papers – reading them and writing them.

> You may think this is a slow and cumbrous way of doing things; but there are two reasons for it. The first is the Parliamentary system of government. Parliament has the right to inquire into any action taken by a Government Department, and a Parliamentary Question may be asked at short notice, perhaps a long time after the event, perhaps in absence of the civil servant who actually took that particular action. So that Parliament may get the information, it is essential that there should be a written record of the action and, as far as possible, of the reasons for it.

> Secondly, the written record is necessary to preserve the impartiality of the Civil Service to the public. The Civil Service cannot, as a private

business sometimes may, give one customer a bargain and make up for it by charging another customer extra; it has to deal with all on the same terms. Therefore, there must be a written record of what has been done in the past, so that it may be done again in the future when the same problem arises. That does not mean that the Civil Service is bound by precedent. Very often there will be no precedent, in other cases it is clearly right to modify earlier policy. But this should be done not by intuition but deliberately after considering what previous practice has been.

Another thing that may strike you is that very few problems seem to be settled by one person alone: the papers may sometimes pass through several hands before a letter is answered or a decision given. This is partly due to the need for looking at the records – a job which is done by the juniors – partly because very often a subject will concern more than one branch of a Department. The process need not cause delay and is essential if there is to be a consistent policy.

From the very first you must learn to be precise and honest in your work. You must fully appreciate the problem to be solved; you must then collect and check all the relevant facts, and set them out clearly and fairly. Don't take anything for granted: there is always more than one point of view, and it may be dangerous to accept somebody else's statement without verifying it for yourself. Don't be lazy and try to pass off a guess as an accurate figure or statement; it may not be questioned, but if it is you must be prepared to justify it. If you see a snag, or a difficulty, or a point which you don't understand, don't ignore it in the hope that nobody else will spot it; it is your job to straighten it out, or if you can't, at least to point it out to your chief and let him deal with it. Whatever shortcomings civil servants may have, they must never be found wanting in this kind of honesty.

Moreover, you must be accurate. You must learn the importance of using words in their exact meanings, so that they convey, to somebody you have never seen, exactly what you intend to convey, and not just something roughly approximating to it. If there is any ambiguity in your phrasing somebody is sure to misunderstand; so say what you mean, simply and clearly. Keep your sentences short and avoid officialese. Read "Plain Words," the book by Sir Ernest Gowers, published by the Stationery Office at 2s[2].

Seventy years later, there is less emphasis on accountability to Parliament and rather more on civil servants' 'first and foremost' duty to serve their departmental Ministers.

There remains, though, significant emphasis on the need for propriety. Here is one commendably brief instruction:

- Don't bend or break the rules

- Put in place and follow clear procedures

- If approval is needed, get it first

- Don't allow a conflict of interest to appear to affect a decision

- Don't use public money for private benefit

- Be even-handed

- Record the reasons for decisions

How did this culture and these rules develop? The rest of this chapter summarises the history of what is often referred to as the Westminster Model of Government. Later chapters go into more detail.

The contents of the rest of this chapter are:

---

[2] '2s' means 2 shillings. Rebecca Gowers, Sir Ernest's great-granddaughter, has created a new edition of 'Plain Words', updating it to reflect modern English usage.

1.2 The UK Constitution

Although often referred to as 'unwritten', most of the UK's constitution is clearly set out in writing. A 2021 blog by David Allen Green[3] provided links to four places where large parts of the constitution can be found, including the *Cabinet Manual*, *The Judge over your Shoulder*, and *Erskine May*.

In short, our constitution attributes power to Parliament, to the Executive, and to the Courts. The relative power of each body varies with the subject matter[4].

The United Kingdom is a Parliamentary (rather than Presidential) democracy. *The Crown in Parliament* is sovereign[5,6].

---

[3]https://www.civilservant.org.uk/library/2021-David-Allen-Green-The_UK's_Written_Constitution.pdf

[4]Citizens' fundamental rights and legal duties do not necessarily derive from Parliamentary enactments. The 2019 Miller Supreme Court judgment on the prorogation of Parliament showed that there can be rare occasions when Parliament is constitutionally so weak that it requires the protection of the courts.

[5]But nothing else done by Parliament is 'sovereign'. For example: a Parliamentary resolution or standing order binds only Parliament (if at all). And statutory instruments can be struck down by the courts as ultra vires the parent Act of Parliament.

[6]Note, too, that there are two sovereignties - Lord Bridge:- "In our society the rule of law rests upon twin foundations: the sovereignty of the Queen in Parliament in making the law and the sovereignty of the Queen's courts in interpreting and applying the law."

[7]A decision by a UK Government to sign an international treaty does not create rights and duties in national law which are enforceable in UK courts. Only UK legislation can create or revoke such rights and duties. European Union law was accordingly incorporated into UK law by the European Communities Act 1972. That legislation could not and did not fetter the ability of successor Parliaments to revoke or amend the 1972 legislation.

An Act of Parliament - following royal assent - is the supreme
law of the land[7].

It would be hard to improve on these words of Lady Hale
and Lord Reed in the UK Supreme Court:

> "Let us remind ourselves of the foundations of our constitution. We live
> in a representative democracy. The House of Commons exists because
> the people have elected its members. The Government is not directly
> elected by the people (unlike the position in some other democracies).
> The Government exists because it has the confidence of the House of
> Commons. It has no democratic legitimacy other than that. This means
> that it is accountable to the House of Commons - and indeed to the
> House of Lords - for its actions, remembering always that the actual
> task of governing is for the executive and not for Parliament or the
> courts."

Put less elegantly:- legitimacy and democracy are main-
tained because Ministers are answerable to Parliament, and
the House of Commons is elected by the people. Subject to
complying with the laws made by Parliament, day to day decisions are taken by Ministers (and if necessary by the whole
Cabinet) and implemented by a politically neutral civil service.

Put shortly, therefore, there is a simple chain of command:

- Civil servants are accountable to Ministers.
- Ministers are accountable to Parliament.
- Members of Parliament are accountable to their constituents.

1.2.1 Edmund Burke and T H Green

Some elements of our modern constitution can be traced back to two influential thinkers. 18th Century philosopher Edmund Burke argued that Members of Parliament (MPs) should act as representatives, not delegates. Burke himself said the following to his constituents, having been returned as an MP:

> "Your representative owes you, not his industry only, but his judgment; and he betrays instead of serving you if he sacrifices it to your opinion."

In other words, MPs should act in what they judge to be the public interest - not as advocates for the interests of their constituents and therefore not necessarily in the way that their constituents might wish them to vote, nor even necessarily in the interests of their own constituency.

(It is worth noting, however, that Burke decided, six years later, that he would not seek re-election rather than lose the forthcoming vote, thus showing that no MP can completely ignore the views of his constituents and hope to be re-elected.)

Building on Burke's model, the 19th Century idealist T H Green described an ethical framework in which civil servants behave with integrity in order to deliver good government. Green argued that, as politicians are inevitably subject to short term and selfish pressures, there needs to be a unified administration in which officials ensure the common good or public interest. To do this, they must be politically neutral and must demonstrate pecuniary and moral integrity. They must not be motivated by the desire to make money. These core values are nowadays described as:

- Integrity
- Honesty
- Objectivity and
- Impartiality – including (again) political impartiality.

The increasing emphasis on political impartiality was then to some extent codified in 1884 when the Gladstone Government determined, in an Order in Council, that 'a civil servant standing for election in a constituency must resign his post when he announces himself as a candidate'.

1.2.2 The Northcote Trevelyan Reforms

The other major 19th Century development was the 1854 Northcote Trevelyan Report[8] on *the Organisation of the Permanent Civil Service*. The authors were responding to pressure for change arising from 'the great and increasing accumulation of public business, and the consequent pressure on the Government.'

The authors recommended that civil servants should be appointed on merit through open competition, rather than patronage.

1.2.3 The Haldane Report

The next major development was the 1918 Haldane Report[9],

---

[8] https://www.civilservant.org.uk/library/1854_Northcote_Trevelyan_Report.pdf
[9] https://www.civilservant.org.uk/library/1918_Haldane_Report.pdf

following the First World War, which recommended the development of deep partnerships between Ministers and officials so as to meet the more complicated requirements of busier government as substantial executive ministries emerged from the first world war.

The report's impact came through two closely-linked ideas:

- Government required investigation and thought in all departments to do its job well: 'continuous acquisition of knowledge and the prosecution of research' were needed "to furnish a proper basis for policy". Gone were the days when key decisions could draw only on the expertise of Ministers, MPs and outside opinion. Ministers could not provide an investigative and thoughtful government on their own. Neither could civil servants, but a partnership between both could do so.

  - Haldane did not spell out how such investigation and thought were to be developed, except to recommend they should be based on a split of functions between government departments which essentially has continued to this day.

- The partnership should be extended from the cluster of officials round a Minister, typical of 19th century government, to embrace whole departments as the repositories of relevant knowledge and opinion.

The relationship between civil servants and Ministers thus became one of mutual interdependence, with Ministers providing authority and officials providing expertise. This 'Haldane Convention' encapsulates the notion that civil servants have an indivisible relationship with their departmental Ministers, quite different to many other models of government around the world, which are often based on separation of powers.

As a result, the UK civil service has no 'constitutional personality' or any responsibility separate from the Government of the day. It is there to provide the Government with advice on the formulation of the policies, to assist in carrying out the Government's decisions, and to manage and deliver Government services. Civil servants therefore ... :

- ... cannot express their own opinions, even in court or in front of a Parliamentary committee,

- ... must loyally carry out Ministers' decisions with precisely the same energy and good will, whether they agree with them or not,

Commentary

Perhaps the most striking thing about Haldane's convention is that there has been no attempt to replace or improve it despite the huge changes that have taken place over the last 100 years. The consequences are quite profound.

The priority attached to political impartiality, for instance, has left little room for non-civil service appointments within government. There may now be more political appointees than in previous years but, even today, the number of such Special Advisers is strictly limited. Ministers do, however, receive much policy and political advice from outside their departments, including from constituents, party members, the media and think tanks.

We have, as result, avoided the problems that are so apparent within the American constitution where 2,000 senior posts are Presidential appointments with the result that many candidates have few relevant qualifications and little relevant experience, and many posts remain open long after the arrival of a new President. The UK system also reduces (but does not entirely eliminate) the dangers of groupthink.

(The UK's approach diverged from the USA immediately after the First World War when President Woodrow Wilson wanted to ensure that, when civil servants exercised discretion, their decisions were the legitimate expression of the President.

UK civil servants are intended to work so closely with Ministers that they know Ministers' minds so well that they take the same decisions that Ministers would take, given the law and the substance of the relevant government policy. This is the reason why civil servants are almost always present when Ministers meet their colleagues to discuss policy and when Ministers meet others in 'official' meetings. They listen into Ministerial phone calls, take notes of meetings and debrief those who need to know. Ministers may not reach decisions in private, with each other or with someone else - nor can officials.

Wilson's alternative approach was to create an administration tied down to the greatest possible extent by detailed rules. Such rules are now published annually and run into thousands of pages. Wilson demanded the greatest possible separation of functions between politicians and officials, the latter taking decisions on specific cases so as to ensure that political interests (and corruption) did not influence administrative decisions. Wilson was an admirer of Northcote-Trevelyan and had hoped to administer government through a wholly merit-based civil service, but the US spoils system was too strong with the result that his separation of functions has been eroded by the politicisation of the top levels of the US executive.

In practice, each part of the federal bureaucracy began to make the rules for itself because politicians did not have the time to do so. And then, as American politicians were also not very interested in holding officials to account, effective accountability was (and remains) to the courts rather than to the President or Congress. All US courts, and particularly the American Supreme Court, appear to be much more 'political' than their UK counterparts.

It appears that the UK may be going the same way. Ministers are increasingly using secondary legislation to implement major policies, whilst the courts seem increasingly drawn into holding the executive to account. The Supreme Court prorogation[10] and Rwanda[11] decisions are perhaps good examples of this.)

Another consequence of Haldane is that civil servants are not allowed to openly support their Minister's policies. It is of course the case that no employee - public or private sector - can expect to be allowed (publicly) to criticise his or her employer's policies. But civil servants aren't allowed to praise them either. This is because the Government's policies might change overnight - under a new Prime Minister, for instance - whereupon previous support for policy A would overnight become seen as criticism of replacement policy B.

It also follows that civil servants cannot be directly questioned about Ministers' policy decisions, thus greatly constraining the effectiveness of Parliamentary inquiries. .

Finally, Manchester University's Dave Richards and York University's Martin Smith offered this interesting analysis:-

… the British system of government is seen to embody a system not of formally codified rules but instead one of advice - determined by the constitutional principle that [Prime] Ministers act as advisers to the sovereign, having in turn been advised by civil servants. It is based on the convention that officials are in a position to advise a Minister on a subject (free from the threat of fear or favour) and as such, there is no requirement for the separation of power between the political and

---

[10] https://www.supremecourt.uk/cases/docs/uksc-2019-0192-summary.pdf
[11] https://www.supremecourt.uk/cases/docs/uksc-2023-0093-press-summary.pdf

administrative class. This is the antithesis of the US 'Wilsonian model' or many other European models of government that are premised on more pluralistic sentiments and a separation of powers.

Constitutionally then, the Haldane convention does not recognise any division in the personality of Ministers and their officials. This principle of both indivisibility and mutual dependence within the UK system is seen as providing both a practical and constitutional constraint to protect against the arbitrary (ab)use of power. This convention became a bedrock of the Westminster model. It established the modus operandi that officials and Ministers should operate in a symbiotic relationship whereby Ministers decide after consultation with their officials whose wisdom, institutional memory and knowledge of the processes of governing helps to guide the Minister. The official is loyal to the Minister who takes the rap when things go wrong. Whatever the problems with this approach, democratic or otherwise, it at least outlined clear lines of responsibility and accountability.

Ministers were the ones held to account even if they often evaded the responsibility. Of course, scratch below the surface and the constitutional niceties of the Minister-civil servant relationship have of course proved at times fractious. The Wilson Government's suspicion and criticism of Whitehall moved it to establish Fulton[12], although infamously of course the Haldane principle was left strictly off-limits. Heath's reorganisations in the early 1970s was an asserted attempt at Ministerial muscle flexing, but Whitehall was not shy in kicking-back. The Benn side-show during the 1970's Labour Government offered some entertaining spats when first in Industry, then in Energy, he challenged the standard operating procedures within Whitehall, so boo-hooing Haldane. But beyond these skirmishes, it is really only since the 1980s, that the Haldane model has been gradually, and largely implicitly, undermined.

This undermining is discussed in the final two chapters of this book.

---

[12] https://www.civilservant.org.uk/csr-fulton_report-findings.html

1.2.4 Crichel Down

This was a 1950s controversy following Prime Minister Winston Churchill's promise that certain land requisitioned for wartime use would be sold back to its former owners after the war. Crichel Down had instead been transferred to the Ministry of Agriculture who greatly increased the price at which they were willing to sell it. The previous owners were furious and the subsequent public inquiry revealed maladministration by civil servants without the knowledge of their Minister. This nevertheless led to the resignation of the Secretary of State for Agriculture (Sir Thomas Dugdale), the first Ministerial resignation since 1917.

The decision of the Minister to resign emphasised the notion that civil servants were ultimately accountable to their Ministers, and the Minister in turn to Parliament, rather than having distinct responsibilities themselves.

The Home Secretary then used the affair to define Ministerial accountability in this way:

- A Minister must protect a civil servant who has carried out an explicit order by the Minister.

- A Minister must protect and defend a civil servant who acts properly in accordance with the policy laid down by the Minister.

- Where an official makes a mistake or causes some delay, but not on an important issue of policy and not where a claim to individual rights is seriously involved, the Minister acknowledges the mistake and accepts the responsibility, although he is not personally involved, and states that he will take appropriate corrective action in the department. The Minister would not expose the official to public criticism.

- Where action has been taken by a civil servant of which the Minister disapproves and has no prior knowledge, and the conduct of the official is reprehensible, there is no obligation on the part of the Minister to endorse what he believes is wrong or to defend what are clearly shown to be errors of his officials. But the Minister remains constitutionally responsible to Parliament for the fact that something has gone wrong, and the Minister alone can tell Parliament what has occurred.

1.3 The Armstrong Memorandum

The (lengthy) Armstrong Memorandum[13], first published in 1985, summarises the duties and responsibilities of civil servants. The most important parts read as follows:

- Civil servants are servants of the Crown. For all practical purposes the Crown in this context means and is represented by the Government of the day. ... The Civil Service as such has no constitutional personality or responsibility separate from the duly constituted Government of the day. It is there to provide the Government of the day with advice on the formulation of the policies of the Government, to assist in carrying out the decisions of the Government, and to manage and deliver the services for which the Government is responsible....

- The Civil Service serves the Government of the day as a whole, that is to say Her Majesty's Ministers collectively, and the Prime Minister is the Minister for the Civil Service. The duty of the individual civil servant is first and foremost to the Minister of the Crown who is in charge of the Department in which he or she is serving.*

---

[13] https://www.civilservant.org.uk/library/1996_Armstrong_Memorandum.pdf

- The basic principles of accountability of Ministers and civil servants are [as follows]:

- Each Minister is responsible to Parliament for the conduct of his Department, and for the actions carried out by his Department in pursuit of Government policies or in the discharge of responsibilities laid upon him as a Minister.

  - A Minister is accountable to Parliament, in the sense that he has a duty to explain in Parliament the exercise of his powers and duties and to give an account to Parliament of what is done by him in his capacity as a Minister or by his Department.

  - Civil servants are responsible to their Ministers for their actions and conduct.

  - The British Civil Service is a non-political and professional career service subject to a code of rules and disciplines. Civil servants are required to serve the duly constituted Government of the day, of whatever political complexion. It is of the first importance that civil servants should conduct themselves in such a way as to deserve and retain the confidence of Ministers, and to be able to establish the same relationship with those whom they may be required to serve in some future Administration. That confidence is the indispensable foundation of a good relationship between Ministers and civil servants. The conduct of civil servants should at all times be such that Ministers and potential future Ministers can be sure that confidence can be freely given, and that the Civil Service will at all times conscientiously fulfil its duties and obligations to, and impartially assist, advise and carry out the policies of, the duly constituted Government of the day.

- The determination of policy is the responsibility of the Minister (within the convention of collective responsibility of the whole Government for the decisions and actions of every member of it).

In the determination of policy the civil servant has no constitutional responsibility or role distinct from that of the Minister. ... It is the
duty of the civil servant to make available to the Minister all the information and experience at his or her disposal which may have a
bearing on the policy decisions to which the Minister is committed
or which he is preparing to make, and to give to the Minister honest and impartial advice, without fear or favour, and whether the
advice accords with the Minister's view or not. Civil servants are
in breach of their duty, and damage their integrity as servants of
the Crown, if they deliberately withhold relevant information from
their Minister, or if they give their Minister other advice than the
best they believe they can give, or if they seek to obstruct or delay
a decision simply because they do not agree with it. When, having
been given all the relevant information and advice, the Minister
has taken a decision, it is the duty of civil servants loyally to carry
out that decision with precisely the same energy and good will,
whether they agree with it or not.

- Civil servants are under an obligation to keep the confidences to
which they become privy in the course of their work; not only the
maintenance of the trust between Ministers and civil servants but
also the efficiency of government depend on their doing so.

- When a civil servant gives evidence to a Select Committee on the
policies or actions of his or her Department, he or she does so as
the representative of the Minister in charge of the Department
and subject to the Minister's instructions ... and is accountable to
the Minister for the evidence which he or she gives. The ultimate
responsibility lies with Ministers, and not with civil servants, to
decide what information should be made available, and how and
when it should be released, whether it is to Parliament, to Select
Committees, to the media or to individuals. It is not acceptable
for a serving or former civil servant to seek to frustrate policies or
decisions of Ministers by the disclosure outside the Government
of information to which he or she has had access as a civil servant.

*It is worth noting that many felt that the second bullet point went too far in down-playing the importance of the Cabinet. Geoffrey Chipperfield , for instance, thought that ...

> '[It was] misleading in its emphasis that, for all practical purposes, the official's boss was his/her Secretary of State. While that was true generally, it downplayed the importance of consensual cabinet agreement and responsibility, and the need, in order to support this, for officials to work with their opposite numbers in other departments and share information. In particular it was important for officials to realize that instructions from their Minister not to consult or share information with other Departments was offending against cabinet government.'

1.4 The Osmotherly Rules

One important element of the Armstrong Memorandum concerns officials giving evidence to Parliament. This instruction must be read in conjunction with the Osmotherly Rules[14], first published a few years earlier in 1980.

Put shortly, officials are allowed to describe and explain the reasons which caused Ministers to adopt existing policies but they should not give information which undermines collective responsibility nor get into a discussion about alternative policies. In particular, they are not allowed to divulge:

- advice given to Ministers by officials;

- information about interdepartmental exchanges on policy issues, the level at which decisions were taken, or the manner in which Ministers consulted their colleagues;

- the private affairs of individuals, including constituents;

---

[14] https://www.civilservant.org.uk/library/2014_Osmotherly_Rules.pdf

- sensitive commercial or economic information, and

- information about negotiations with other governments or bodies such as the European Commission.

When a civil servant gives evidence to a Select Committee on the policies or actions of his or her Department, he or she does so as the representative of the Minister in charge of the Department and subject to the Minister's instructions ... and is accountable to the Minister for the evidence which he or she gives. The ultimate responsibility lies with Ministers, and not with civil servants, to decide what information should be made available, and how and when it should be released, whether it is to Parliament, to Select Committees, to the media or to individuals.

Note, however, that senior officials have recently become entitled to refuse to sign off plans which they regard as unrealistic, and they are held directly accountable for the successful delivery of those plans which they have signed off as realistic. Further information is in chapter 6.

1.5 The Carltona Principle

This is the legal principle under which civil servants exercise power on behalf of Ministers. Secretaries of State (etc.) are responsible for the way in which their decisions are exercised by their officials, but they are not required to have attended personally to every one of them.

The case most often cited as authority for the proposition that a person may authorise another to exercise a power for and on his or her behalf is Carltona Ltd v Commissioners of Works 1943. This was a wartime dispute dealing with the requisition by the Government of a factory which manufactured food products. In Carltona, the English Court of Appeal considered whether a Minister had to exercise personally a power to take possession of land, or whether the power could be exercised by one of the Minister's departmental officials for and on behalf of the Minister. The court concluded that the power in question could be exercised by a departmental official for and on behalf of the Minister. The court's reasoning indicates that there are two grounds which justify a Minister being able to authorise an officer to exercise a power vested in the Minister:

- the Minister is ultimately responsible to Parliament for the decision of an authorised officer; and

- in modern government, Ministers have so many functions and powers that administrative necessity dictates that they act through duly authorised officers.

Note, however, that this principle was eroded somewhat by the 2020 decision that the imprisonment of former leader of Sinn Fein, Gerry Adams, had been unlawful because it had been approved by a junior Minister instead of by the Secretary of State in person. The longer term consequences of this decision remain to be seen.

Note also that a person exercising a power for and on behalf of another does so as the 'agent' or 'alter ego' of the person in whom the power is vested. The act of the authorised person is therefore, at law, the act of the person in whom the power is vested. This is fundamentally different to the act of a delegate which, at law, is the delegate's and not the delegator's act.

1.6 The Seven Principles of Public Life ('The Nolan Principles')

The Seven Principles of Public Life were promulgated in 1995 by Lord Nolan in the first report of *the Committee on Standards in Public Life*. They encapsulate the values and behaviour appropriate to the whole of the public sector, and apply as much to the civil service as to other holders of public office.

- Selflessness:- Holders of public office should take decisions solely in terms of the public interest. They should not do so in order to gain financial or other material benefits for themselves, their families or their friends.

- Integrity:- Holders of public office should not place themselves under any financial or other obligation to outside individuals or organisations that might influence them in the performance of their official duties.

- Objectivity:- In carrying out public business, including making public appointments, awarding contracts, or recommending individuals for rewards or benefits, holders of public office should make choices on merit.

- Accountability:- Holders of public office are accountable for their decisions and actions to the public and must submit themselves to whatever scrutiny is appropriate to their office.

- Openness:- Holders of public office should be as open as possible about the decisions and actions that they take. They should give reasons for their decisions and restrict information only when the wider public interest clearly demands.

- Honesty:- Holders of public office have a duty to declare any private interests relating to their public duties and to take steps to resolve any conflicts arising in a way that protects the public interest.

- Leadership:- Holders of public office should promote and support these principles by leadership and example.

The Civil Service Code

Much of the above is brought together in the Civil Service Code[15],[16] which was first published in 1996. This important document is discussed in great detail in chapters 2 and 3.

The code was later given legal force by *the Constitutional Reform and Governance Act 2010* (The CRaG Act).

1.7 Ministers' Duties

Ministers owe these three important duties to their civil servants:

First, Ministers may not ask civil servants to do things which are illegal or improper (such as spending public money without proper approval).

Second, they must consider officials' advice, even if they do not take it. They cannot therefore take a policy decision without first giving officials an opportunity to advise them on the

---

[15] https://www.civilservant.org.uk/library/2015_civil_service_code.pdf
[16] There are slightly different versions for the Home Civil Service, the Diplomatic Service, and the Devolved Administrations - Scotland, Wales and Northern Ireland.

suitability of their proposed course of action. The Ministerial Code[17] says that 'Ministers have a duty to give fair consideration and due weight to informed and impartial advice from civil servants'.

Third, Ministers may not ask officials to hide information from other interested officials, nor from Cabinet Ministers, in their own or other departments, nor may they ask officials to help circumvent collective discussion, for instance by announcing a 'decision' whilst a Cabinet colleague remains opposed to it.

This third duty is important because it underpins collective Cabinet government. Ministers often compete with one another as they seek promotion or when promoting their pet policies. But the quality of policy- and decision-making quickly deteriorates if Cabinet colleagues - and in particular the Chancellor and No.10 - are kept in the dark.

It is of course sometimes sensible to work up a proposal before showing it to colleagues. But officials may not collude in a 'bounce' and if they feel that colleagues in another department would expect to be told about a proposal, then they must tell them. Civil servants may therefore not support free-lancing – actions of individual Ministers or small groups that do not have the sanction of the government as a whole. But officials may support the Prime Minister if (s)he wishes to establish a small secret group to focus on a sensitive issue.

It is also worth noting that the Ministerial Code says that Ministers have an overarching duty 'to comply with the law'.

[17] https://www.civilservant.org.uk/library/2019-MINISTERIAL-CODE-FINAL.pdf

A reference to 'international law' was removed during one update of the code but the Cabinet Office, when challenged, said that the previous reference to international law had been unnecessary as it was subsumed within the definition of law. (There is more on this is Chapter 2.2.8.1.)

1.8 Official Guidance & Further Reading

The indivisibility and mutual dependence of Minsters and civil servants mean that officials must also work within the laws, conventions and rules summarised in:

- The Cabinet Manual[18],
- The Ministerial Code[19], and
- The Civil Service Code[20].

Civil servants are employed by the Crown under *the Royal Prerogative*[21] and powers delegated under the Prerogative and under various Acts, regulations, instructions etc. The most important of these are:

- the Civil Service Order in Council 1991,
- the Civil Service (Management Functions) Act 1992,
- the Civil Service Order in Council 1995, and
- the Civil Service Management Code (which includes the Civil Service Code).

Further information about the Orders in Council etc. may be obtained from the Government's official Civil Service website.

---

[18] https://www.civilservant.org.uk/library/2011_cabinet-manual.pdf
[19] https://www.civilservant.org.uk/library/2010_Ministerial_Code.pdf
[20] https://www.civilservant.org.uk/library/2015_civil_service_code.pdf
[21] https://www.civilservant.org.uk/skills-parliamentary_business.html

BACKGROUND, HISTORY & FURTHER READING   25

There is good general guidance in "Propriety and Audit in the Public Sector[22]" published by the NAO-chaired Public Audit Forum in August 2001.

Lady Hale's 2017 speech *The UK Constitution on the Move*[23] includes a very nice summary of the UK constitution, although she doesn't touch on the role of the Civil Service.

Detailed guidance is available in the following documents, all of which are on the Cabinet Office or Treasury web sites.

Cabinet Office

- Civil Service Management Code:- addressed to central government departments and agencies and setting out the terms and conditions on which civil servants are to be employed

- Standards of Propriety:- also addressed to central government departments and agencies, this document covers subjects such as the requirement of staff to seek permission before accepting outside hospitality, and the sale of surplus property to civil servants.

- Guidance for Civil Servants: an interesting and readable two volume Directory of Civil Service Guidance

HM Treasury

- Regularity and Propriety[24] is a handbook written mainly for Accounting Officers but offering a readable summary of what is and is not "proper" behaviour in the stewardship of public funds

- The Accounting Officer's Survival Guide[25] is intended to help new Accounting Officers understand their personal responsibilities and to help established Accounting Officers resolve problems arising.

---

[22] https://www.civilservant.org.uk/library/2001_propriety_audit.pdf
[23] https://www.civilservant.org.uk/library/2017-Lady_Hale-The_UK_Constitution_on_the_Move.pdf
[24] https://www.civilservant.org.uk/library/2004_Regularity_Propriety_VFM.pdf
[25] https://www.civilservant.org.uk/library/2015-HMT-occounting_officer's_survival_guide.pdf

- Government Accounting

- DAO letters: (Dear Accounting Officer letters)

- Procurement Guidance

- The Sharman Report: "The Review of Audit and Accountability for Central Government, February 2001.

Further Reading

Douglas Wass' 1983 Reith Lecture 'The Privileged Adviser[26]' is a highly readable review of the relationship between Minister and senior official as it was then, and as it is still supposed to be.

An excellent summary of the constitutional development of the UK Civil Service through to 1997 may be found in Michael Duggett's paper The Evolution of the UK Civil Service[27].

---

[26] https://www.civilservant.org.uk/library/1983_reith3.pdf
[27] https://www.civilservant.org.uk/library/1997_evolution_1848-1997.pdf

Chapter 2
Civil Service Ethics

Contents

2.1 The Civil Service Code[28]

The Civil Service Code provides a clear, and commendably brief summary of the values that are common to all civil servants of all grades and in all departments, and the standards of behaviour that are expected of them. This chapter, and the next, explain what the code means in practical terms.

The key parts of this text were checked for accuracy by the Cabinet Office in 2000 but it has occasionally been suggested that we now live in different times. One correspondent wondered "if some people might nevertheless read the material on impartiality and ethics somewhat cynically, given the way senior civil servants have become more politicised in recent years, and especially in the light of today's No 10 shenanigans? Some might argue that the rules, and application of them, are lagging behind the realities of the way that senior civil servants [are required to] operate." My short answer is that no-one in authority, such as a Minister or senior Cabinet Office official, has ever suggested that civil servants' constitutional role or ethical responsibilities have changed since 2000, or that anything in this text is wrong. Until they do so, clearly and unequivocally, I believe that the following advice remains accurate.

---

[28] The first version of this Code of Practice was put in place in January 1996 at the suggestion of the then Treasury and Civil Service Select Committee, and was revised in May 1999 to take account of devolution to Scotland and Wales. A significantly new edition was published in June 2006. It differed from the previous one in two main ways:
- If a civil servant believes that that he/she is being asked to behave in a way which conflicts with the code, he/she may now report the matter direct to the Civil Service Commissioners.
- It is now clearly specified that the code is part of the contractual relationship between the civil servant and his/her employer.
The code has since been amended several times but its substance has remained essentially unchanged.

The code's introduction reads as follows (emphasis added):

> The Civil Service is an integral and key part of the government of the United Kingdom. It supports the Government of the day in developing and implementing its policies, and in delivering public services. Civil servants are accountable to Ministers, who in turn are accountable to Parliament.
>
> As a civil servant, *you are appointed on merit on the basis of fair and open competition* and are expected to carry out your role with dedication and a commitment to the Civil Service and its core values: *integrity, honesty, objectivity and impartiality*.

The code defines civil servants' four core values in the following way:

- '**integrity**' is putting the obligations of public service above your own personal interests;

- '**honesty**' is being truthful and open;

- '**objectivity**' is basing your advice and decisions on rigorous analysis of the evidence; and

- '**impartiality**' is acting solely according to the merits of the case and serving equally well Governments of different political persuasions.

> These core values are intended to "support good government and ensure the achievement of the highest possible standards in all that the Civil Service does. This in turn helps the Civil Service to gain and retain the respect of Ministers, Parliament, the public and its customers."

The code itself helpfully defines integrity, honesty etc. in more detail. Let's look at each one, and also appointment on merit and accountability, and consider the practical consequences for civil servants.

2.2 Integrity

I like this brief definition of integrity:

Integrity is choosing your thoughts and actions based on values rather than personal gain.

I also like this simple rule governing your spending of public funds:

All expenditure must be **R**equired, **R**easonable and **R**eceipted.

The code does into more detail:

You must:

- fulfil your duties and obligations responsibly;

- always act in a way that is professional and that deserves and retains the confidence of all those with whom you have dealings;

- carry out your fiduciary obligations responsibly (that is make sure public money and other resources are used properly and efficiently);

- deal with the public and their affairs fairly, efficiently, promptly, effectively and sensitively, to the best of your ability;

- keep accurate official records and handle information as openly as possible within the legal framework; and

- comply with the law and uphold the administration of justice.

You must not:

- misuse your official position, for example by using information acquired in the course of your official duties to further your private interests or those of others;

- accept gifts or hospitality or receive other benefits from anyone which might reasonably be seen to compromise your personal judgement or integrity; or

- disclose official information without authority. This duty continues to apply after you leave the Civil Service.

A wider definition of integrity would require you to intervene if you were to see somebody doing something wrong. If that were not possible then you would publicise the bad behaviour and/or leave the compromised organisation. But it is unfortunately difficult (and often wrong) for civil servants to take such a principled stand against behaviour which the official regards as 'wrong' but which has implicitly or specifically been approved by democratically appointed and accountable politicians. The implications of this are discussed in detail in Chapter 4 ("No! Minister").

That aside ...

What does integrity mean in practice?

2.2.1 Conflicts of interest

Great care needs to be taken to avoid conflicts of interest, whether real or perceived. You may be certain that you could rise above them, but others will doubt it. Indeed, much administrative law (i.e. judicial review) is concerned with conflicts of interest.

All potential conflicts of interest, including conflicts with the interests of your immediate family, must therefore be disclosed to managers, remembering that an innocuous friendship, investment, gift or treat can be transformed overnight into a possible conflict of interest. The following paragraphs provide guidance, but nothing in them should be taken to detract from departmental guidance, which should be consulted, and taken to prevail, in case of doubt. Indeed, certain individual departments, or parts of departments, have additional requirements above those mentioned below.

2.2.2 Gifts, Hospitality etc.

These may be divided into three categories.

First, there are gifts from a company whose services you are using or might use, or with whom you might negotiate grant or other support, or which might materially benefit from decisions with which you might be involved. There are absolutely no circumstances in which you can accept a gift of any value, or any hospitality more substantial than a working lunch, from such a source.

Second, expensive gifts (each department defines its own limit) from other donors must also generally be refused or returned. Alternatively, it is sometimes possible to say to the donor 'Thank you for the gift which I will use in the office rather than for my personal use'. (You can donate wine to the Christmas party.) Failing this, you can hand the gift over to the department, or pay the department to let you keep it.

Third, any gifts, hospitality etc. whose acceptance is not prohibited under the first two rules above, should also be refused unless the acceptance can clearly be justified as contributing to the achievement of your objectives. Put another way, the reason for the acceptance has to be clearly defensible, always remembering the Greek proverb that 'gifts are poison'.

Positive reasons for accepting hospitality include the need to carry out an ambassadorial role, make contacts and gain information. It is therefore generally OK to attend celebrations of a company's success or longevity, or an industry-wide gathering, including trade association dinners. It is also reasonable to accept inexpensive gifts such as ties and pens, so as to avoid giving offence.

Conversely, it is important to avoid developing a sense of obligation to a host or donor, and to avoid criticism (from those unable to benefit) of benefiting from lavish hospitality etc. In general, therefore, you should not accept tickets for major sporting events, Glyndebourne or Covent Garden. It is seldom a good argument that you are establishing or maintaining contacts at such events, because it is seldom appropriate or possible to discuss business.

It is often useful to apply the 'wow' test. When you receive an invitation and find yourself saying 'wow' then it is time to refuse.

A similar approach should be adopted when considering whether you might be accompanied by a partner to an event. Indeed, the negative factors can be more intense, given that the cost to the host will have doubled, and the opportunity to do business will have diminished. On the other hand, it can be helpful to be accompanied by a partner to an event at which you are trying to build up a relationship with the host or to an event at which you are acting as an ambassador, for instance at a company celebration or an event in aid of charity.

It is usually acceptable to accept local transport, lunch and refreshments when visiting private sector companies. But you may never let a private sector company pay your rail fare, air fare or overnight hotel bill. It is also acceptable to accept overnight accommodation in a company's guest house provided for that purpose, but of course you must not then claim the cost of a hotel. And it is permissible to accept a free flight in a company plane if there is no convenient public transport and if the plane would have been making the journey anyway. But the offer of such transport should be refused if convenient public transport is available, or if the provision of the flight would cause the company to incur significant expense.

Incidentally, the NAO published a report, in early 2016, on the acceptance of gifts etc. In general, the NAO found that the above rules were being observed, but they did criticise the acceptance of tickets to professional sports and cultural events, sometimes accompanied by a spouse and/or children; bottles of champagne; wine for a team's Christmas lunch; and iPads. You have been warned!

2.2.3 Financial Interests

We must all take particular care to avoid profiting, or enabling others to profit, (or even getting into a position where we could do these things) from information which is supplied to us in confidence. In particular, you must consult your line manager if you are asked to handle papers concerning any company (including a bank) in which you have invested, or with which you have any financial link. (However, standard bank accounts may be ignored for this purpose, unless they contain a huge amount of money.) You must also tell your manager if you hold shares in, or have any other link with, any company which is dealt with by you or your colleagues. You must do this immediately on joining the team, or immediately on acquiring the shares etc. This applies even if the shares are held via a vehicle such as an ISA. Holdings in collective vehicles such as OEICs need not be reported unless you have a large holding and you know that your money has invested in a company or companies with which you are dealing.

2.2.4 Outside Appointments, Employments and Other Interests

You must tell your line manager in advance, or on appointment, about any other employment or self-employment. You must also disclose links to all other bodies (including charities) if it looks as though you might be asked to deal with them on behalf of your department or if your involvement might be time-consuming.

Having done this, you should find that most outside appointments and employments are absolutely fine as long as they do not take up time which should be devoted to your employment in the civil service. Indeed, they are often encouraged as a means of broadening your experience. The Business Department, for instance, will often encourage senior staff to become non-executive directors so as to gain experience of business. And Department of Education staff would gain much valuable experience if they were to become school governors.

Again subject to notifying your line manager, it is generally OK to write articles and make speeches etc. on non-work related subjects - as long as you prepare for such activities outside working hours.

2.2.5 Post-Retirement Business Appointments

It is obviously important that there should be no cause for any suspicion of impropriety when you take up a new job after retirement. This is mainly to ensure that you do not treat the companies favourably because you thought you might be rewarded when you were no longer a civil servant.

All offers of employment should therefore be reported to your department who will if necessary involve the Advisory Committee on Business Appointments (ACOBA) which gives advice on applications at the most senior levels, and reviews a wider sample in order to ensure consistency and effectiveness.

Sadly, however, ACOBA has no power other than to give advice, and there have been numerous examples of senior figures, including ex-Ministers, accepting high profile appointments well in advance of seeking clearance.

2.2.6 Fraud and Corruption

Criminal corruption - such as accepting bribes or rigging contracts - is vanishingly rare in the UK civil service. Indeed, I know of no examples. This is in large part due to the all-pervasive and self-policing ethical culture. It also helps that civil servants' salaries are close to market rates so officials generally don't feel cheated by their employer.

Fraud is also very uncommon, though not unknown.

- Edward Chapman in effect stole around £1 million before his mother - also a civil servant - found out about it and informed the authorities. Chapman was jailed for three years in 2016. This was hardly classic corruption as Chapman had no accomplices.

- Alan Williams defrauded his department of £1.7 million between 2017 and 2019 before a colleague became suspicious. Again, there were no accomplices - he simply set up a bogus company and contract, using his knowledge of financial controls to circumvent them. He was jailed for three and a half years.

Daniel Finkelstein, writing in The Times, explained why both civil servants and Ministers must expect heavy punishment when they are dishonest:

> In his excellent book *Lying for Money* Dan Davies investigates large-scale fraud and how the perpetrators manage, at least initially, to get away with it. Common to many of these crimes is that the fraudster has corrupted someone who belongs to what Davies calls the "circle of trust". They have managed to persuade someone who is an accountant, a lawyer or an actuary to become a confederate.
>
> Davies explains the economics of this. The professionals in the circle of trust are expensive to corrupt, because they are well-paid people with a lot to lose. They have spent years training and if found guilty of an offence by a disciplinary panel they lose all the financial advantages their qualifications have bought them. Because everyone knows it is difficult and pricey to "turn" a professional, they tend to be trusted. And this makes fraudulent professionals devastatingly effective. The status, the trust, the price, the fraud, the disciplinary system are all locked together.
>
> For this reason, it is vital the people in the circle of trust are subject to harsh discipline for even minor infractions. Exceptionally tough punishment for what looks like almost irrelevant pieces of dishonesty is what keeps the whole system working. That is why the disciplinary panel dismissed [PC] Simon Read in a kerfuffle about a box of doughnuts. It is about maintaining the system of trust that avoids serious fraud.
>
> The prime minister of the country must be someone inside the circle of trust. Someone that people appreciate has so much to lose that they will abide by the rules and tell the truth in all circumstances. There are so many parts of our governing system that depend upon most people accepting the basic integrity of the occupant of No 10.
>
> The apparent disproportion between the office of a prime minister and the issue of a cheese and wine party is not an argument against resignation. Because the real issue is the maintenance of trust in the office, and the fact that removing a prime minister is almost unthinkable is essential to that trust.

2.2.7 Institutional Integrity

The vast majority of civil servants have a pretty good idea of what it means to behave with integrity as individuals. I am less sure that we collectively ensure that our departments act with integrity. Do they (as required by the Civil Service Code):

- always act in a way that is professional and that deserves and retains the confidence of all those with whom they have dealings;

- carry out their fiduciary obligations responsibly (that is make sure public money and other resources are used properly and efficiently);

- deal with the public and their affairs fairly, efficiently, promptly, effectively and sensitively, to the best of their ability;

- keep accurate official records and handle information as openly as possible within the legal framework; and

- comply with the law and uphold the administration of justice?

The civil service is, after all, just as prone as other large organisations to start acting in its own self-interest rather than the wider public good. Many senior managers do not know (and sometimes do not want to know) what is going on in local establishments such as hospitals and prisons. The perennial difficulty of speaking truth to power[29], compounded by the incentive to report good results, also means that even well-motivated senior managers are often the last to learn what is going wrong. Herd behaviour and groupthink are also surprisingly common and exacerbate the culture and tensions that are typical of most large organisations.

---

[29] https://www.civilservant.org.uk/richborne_publishing.html#STtP

Whole departments are therefore sometimes accused lacking integrity - for instance in their dealings with immigrants - see the Windrush scandal. And the Department of Health was shown to have presided over a dysfunctional local health service and regulators in the report into deaths at the Gosport War Memorial Hospital:

> "Over the many years during which the families have sought answers to their legitimate questions and concerns, they have been repeatedly frustrated by senior figures. ... The obfuscation by those in authority has often made the relatives of those who died angry and disillusioned. ... The records show that the Department of Health used a number of different Freedom of Information Act exemptions to resist publication of the Baker Report until legal advice was received in July 2013 that it should be published."

I am pretty sure, too, that a good number of departments fail to deal efficiently and promptly with the public, and fail to keep accurate official records. I understand that it is proving particularly hard to access electronic records in some departments. More generally, there is a good deal of evidence that the 21st Century civil service now devotes too much effort to defending Ministerial policies and devotes too little effort to speaking truth to power. The Cabinet Office, for instance, led some pretty determined resistance to freedom of information requests which might embarrass the government. A Bulgarian official was quoted as saying that "in Britain [your] corruption is so sophisticated that cunning people can deny its existence".

It will be interesting, in years to come, to see how later

generations and historians view our current struggles with these issues.

2.2.8 Compliance with the Law

It is well accepted that some laws cannot, or should not, be fully enforced against citizens. HMRC, for instance, maintains a substantial list of current or previous *extra-statutory concessions:-* "relaxations which give taxpayers a reduction in tax liability to which they would not be entitled under the strict letter of the law."

On a rather larger scale, eyebrows were raised when Ministers ordered HMRC to 'prioritise the flow of goods into the UK over compliance with customs regulations' because the department's systems were not yet ready when the UK left the European Union on 31 January 2020. HMRC accepted that 'some compliance risks' would arise as a result, and that the UK would probably lose £800m in customs duty and VAT in 2021[30]. This failure to properly apply the law was nevertheless accepted as a reasonably pragmatic step which did not raise ethical questions for officials.

But civil servants must not ignore or seek to circumvent laws which confer rights upon UK citizens. **The Civil Service Code says that civil servants must 'comply with the law and uphold the administration of justice'.**

This obligation (and the other Civil Service Code obligations) were incorporated into civil servants' terms and conditions

---

[30] Public Accounts Committee c.21 January 2021

of employment by the Constitutional Reform and Governance (CRaG) Act[31].

2.2.8.1 International Law

Should civil servants accept instructions which are incompatible with international law? The majority of lawyers experienced in these fields suggest that the answer is 'No' – they should not.

This extends to officials' duty to comply with any interim measures imposed by international courts in advance of their final decisions. The leading case is *Mamatkulov and Askarov v. Turkey* which held that any failure to comply with interim measures would frustrate obligations and rights provided in the relevant international treaty.

The fundamental point is that civil servants are required (under their Code and the CraG Act) to "comply with the law" and that means every law, not just most of them. I and others fail to see how those employed in areas subject to international law can avoid complying with that law. In addition, of course, the Ministerial Codes (in both Westminster and Belfast) are very clear that Ministers may not ask civil servants to do things which are illegal or improper. (See also chapter 4.4.)

Here is a brief history of the debate.

The status of international law was considered when an amended Ministerial Code was published in 2015. This (still)

---

[31] https://www.legislation.gov.uk/ukpga/2010/25/contents

required Ministers to obey the law, but omitted previous versions' references to the need to obey international law. The Cabinet Office itself did not draw attention to this potentially significant change, but responded, on being challenged, that the previous reference to international law had been unnecessary as it was subsumed within the definition of law.

This point was expressly considered in *R (Gulf Centre for Human Rights) v (1) The Prime Minister and (2) The Chancellor of the Duchy of Lancaster [2018] EWCA Civ 1855*. The key text is in paras 19-22 where the Court of Appeal held that the reference to "international law and treaty obligations" in the previous (2010) Ministerial Code had been subsumed within the stated duty "to comply with the law" ... they are not independent obligations but simply part of the "overarching" duty of compliance with the law. ... the reference to the duty "to comply with the law" in the 2015 Code is general and unqualified. In so far as that duty includes international law and treaty obligations, they are so included. It is not necessary for there to be specific inclusive language."

As noted in Chapter 4.4, there have been very few examples of civil servants ever being asked to do something illegal ... until 2020 when the Johnson government tabled the *Internal Market Bill* some of whose provisions - if enacted - would have conflicted with international law in the form of *the Brexit Withdrawal Agreement*. Clause 45 of the Bill provided that "The following [various regulations etc.] have effect notwithstanding any relevant international or domestic law with which they may be incompatible or inconsistent …". The Bill drew much criticism and opposition as it made its way through Parliament and the controversial provisions were withdrawn from the Bill.

The Cabinet Secretary determined (correctly in my view) that civil servants could not refuse to help draft the Bill. It was far less certain that they could have implemented the provisions of the Act (if it had become law) and so contravene international law. The same principles apply to the distinction between drafting and implementing the Rwanda legislation - see further below.

Following publication of *the Internal Market Bill*, there was a lively Twitter debate in October 2021 where one lawyer argued that international law is in some ways dissimilar to domestic law and (if I understood correctly) applies only to states (such as the UK) and not to individuals within those states. The UK as a whole might therefore breach international law, but its civil servants could not. I did not find the argument 100% persuasive and – more importantly – neither did those experienced international and constitutional lawyers who joined the debate.

A deeper and longer analysis of the debate (though not dealing with the role of civil servants) may be found in David Allen Green's 'The Law and Policy Blog' published on 12 October 2021. In short, he argued that the UK government was not about to breach the Northern Irish protocol by accident or through recklessness, or on the basis of a grey area of interpretation. It intended to deliberately breach the Northern Irish protocol by using domestic legislation. This was, in essence, the United Kingdom government asserting that a legal obligation did not bind it. This would be a fundamental repudiation of the general principle that a legal command should be obeyed.

The legal position was then tested in 2022 when Northern Ireland Minister Edwin Poots demanded that officials stop building the Border Control Posts required by the UK/EU Northern Ireland Protocol. Mr Poots' Permanent Secretary told Stormont's Agricultural Committee that he was "absolutely required to comply with the law ... I am accountable to the Minister generally, but in this case I am acting against the Minister's wishes." The Northern Ireland courts agreed. A judge ruled that "There shouldn't be any doubt or confusion hanging over those civil servants who have to comply with the law. I propose to make an order, suspending the order or instruction given by the Minister for Agriculture until further order of this court or completion of these proceedings".

There was an interesting exchange in the House of Lords Constitution Committee on 28 June 2023. Attorney General Victoria Prentis agreed that "the rule of law requires compliance by the state with its obligations in international law". The above-mentioned change in the Ministerial Code was then brought to her attention and she agreed that the Government had confirmed in litigation that, nevertheless, the reference to the rule of law included the rule of law in the sphere of international law.

Ms Prentis was rather more cagey when questioned about her role if there were ever a serious conflict between domestic law (which can be altered by Parliament) and an international law obligation of the UK. Commenting later, George Peretz KC said that her reluctance to be pinned down reminded him of a Private Secretary in "Yes Minister" when asked whether, when the chips were down, he'd be loyal to his Minister or to the civil service. "My job", he said, "is to see that the chips stay up".

Then came the December 2023 draft Safety of Rwanda (Asylum and Immigration) Bill which contains quite dramatic 'notwithstanding' (or 'ouster') provisions which purport to disapply large swathes of international law. Crucially, however, it does not disapply the CRaG Act and so does not remove civil servants' duty to comply with international law. Here are extracts from Joshua Rozenberg's commentary (emphasis added) drawing on the views of Mark Elliott, Professor of Public Law at the University of Cambridge.

> What clause 1 is trying to establish is that removing a "relocated individual" to Rwanda once the Rwanda treaty has been ratified would not be a breach of international law. But there is an obvious flaw in this proposition. **Parliament makes national law but not international law.** Simply saying something is in compliance with international law does not make it so. The most that this legislation can do is to stop the courts of the United Kingdom finding removals to Rwanda unlawful. It cannot affect the UK's international treaty obligations.
>
> …
>
> Subsection (2) says: It is for a Minister of the Crown (and only a Minister of the Crown) to decide whether the United Kingdom will comply

with [interim measures]. ... there is no escaping what this stark subsection means. A junior minister, on behalf of the United Kingdom, may choose to break what the court responsible for its enforcement regards as a binding provision of international law. **The minister would be acting lawfully — but His Majesty's government would not**.

After all, he explains, this bill is "an affront to the separation of powers and the rule of law, in that it effectively reverses a Supreme Court judgment, undermines the judicial function and attempts to remove from the courts' jurisdiction questions about the legality of government decisions. In orthodoxy, the principle of parliamentary sovereignty — which makes whatever parliament enacts lawful — would be a complete answer to these charges. But, in *Privacy International*[32], Lord Carnwath said **"it is ultimately for the courts, not the legislature, to determine the limits set by the rule of law to the power to exclude review"**. For a court to take the step implied in this comment — by holding, in effect, that parliament had exceeded its authority by seeking to limits the courts' constitutional role — would be fraught with risk for the judiciary. **It is, however, conceivable that the Rwanda Bill might transform what has largely remained a hypothetical question about the fundamental relationship between parliament and the courts into a live one.**

Ultimately, [Professor Elliot] believes [that] the Rwanda Bill "proceeds on the basis of the sleight of hand that the UK parliament, because it is sovereign, can somehow free the government from its international legal obligations. But this is to conflate the sovereignty of the UK parliament in domestic law with the UK's sovereignty on the international plane as a state. It is precisely in exercise of its state sovereignty that the UK can enter, and has entered, into binding treaty obligations. The peculiarity that the UK's parliament, as a matter of domestic law, is sovereign in the sense of being (in orthodoxy, at least) beyond judicial control cuts no ice whatever on the international level.

---

[32] https://www.supremecourt.uk/cases/docs/uksc-2018-0004-press-summary.pdf

The Cabinet Office, in January 2024, instructed civil servants what they should do if they were to become aware of a 'Rule 39' interim order issued by the European Court of Human rights which required the UK to defer removal of an asylum seeker to Rwanda. The previous position was removal should immediately be deferred. As from January 2024, Home Office case workers are required immediately to refer the case for a ministerial decision whether or not to proceed with removal. Officials would then be expected to "proceed with removal if the minister approves that course of action".

The Cabinet Office did not, however, address the obvious conflict between civil servants' duty to comply with ministerial instructions and their duty to comply with international law. This conflict would need to be drawn to the attention of Ministers, and the Attorney General would need to get involved in the decision making. For the moment, therefore, Cabinet Office officials appear to be following the lead of the Attorney General (as described by George Peretz, above) by doing what they can to ensure 'that the chips stay up'.

2.3 Honesty and Objectivity

The code says that:

You must: set out the facts and relevant issues truthfully, and correct any errors as soon as possible; and use resources only for the authorised public purposes for which they are provided.

You must not: deceive or knowingly mislead Ministers, Parliament or others; or be influenced by improper pressures from others or the prospect of personal gain.

You must: provide information and advice, including advice to Ministers, on the basis of the evidence, and accurately present the options and facts; take decisions on the merits of the case; and take due account of expert and professional advice.

You must not: ignore inconvenient facts or relevant considerations when providing advice or making decisions; or frustrate the implementation of policies once decisions are taken by declining to take, or abstaining from, action which flows from those decisions.

What does this mean in practice?

This is constitutionally perhaps the most important part of the code. A civil service that lies to the public or to Parliament must clearly be reckoned to be a failed institution. Civil servants must refuse to take part in any activity that involves telling lies to anyone, or involves misrepresentation to Parliament.

Officials should not bend to ministerial or other pressure to give credence to scientific illiteracy, conspiracy theories or 'alternative facts'. They should aim to communicate what reputable journalists refer to as 'the best obtainable version of the truth'. If a Minister or Spad wants to stray beyond this then they should take personal responsibility for their statement.

It can be helpful, if challenged about your respect for verifiable facts, to repeat Hannah Arendt's story about Georges Clemenceau. He was asked, after the end of the First World War, who had been responsible for starting it. He replied: "I don't know. But I know for certain they will not say that Belgium invaded Germany."

Officials may not, in particular, transmit to Parliament an answer to a Parliamentary Question or any other information which they believe to be inaccurate or misleading. But officials are not under any obligation to correct a Minister's misrepresentation, whether deliberate or otherwise.

(There may be exceptions to the above rules if national security is threatened, but these are never of concern to the vast majority of civil servants.)

Is this part of the Civil Service Code ever breached? I think the problem is not that officials fail to tell the truth, but some of them are adept at failing to tell the whole truth, and maybe nothing but the truth. I deal with these issues in part 2.2.7 above (institutional integrity) and chapter 3 - political impartiality.

2.4 Personal Impartiality

The Civil Service Code has separate advice on 'impartiality' and 'political impartiality'. In order to highlight the difference, I refer to them as 'personal' and 'political' impartiality.

The code says this on personal impartiality:

You must: carry out your responsibilities in a way that is fair, just and equitable and reflects the Civil Service commitment to equality and diversity.

You must not: act in a way that unjustifiably favours or discriminates against particular individuals or interests.

What does this mean in practice?

The public expect both Ministers and their officials to deal equally with everyone, and with every organisation, without prejudice, favour or disfavour. This simple but vital concept has a number of useful consequences.

First, it enables you to ask appropriate questions, however grand the person or organisation with which you are dealing. For instance, an enquiry into the financial standing of a multinational can often be less rigorous than a similar enquiry of a small firm. But large firms and substantial charities can go bust (remember *Kids Company*), so you should never take anything for granted. Ask a carefully targeted question and then decide whether further questions are necessary. Take particular care if you have heard a critical rumour or comment. There can be smoke without fire, but the two are usually closely associated.

Second, it is your defence against the senior or public figure who might otherwise expect you to give them priority, or rubber stamp some sort of application. You must never allow queue-jumping, nor must you ever refrain from asking a pertinent question, whoever you are dealing with.

It is of course perfectly reasonable to 'fast track' some work for a senior person who has a genuine need for it to be done quickly. But you must be sure that you would do the same for anyone else with a similar need, and that they are not jumping ahead of someone whose needs are just as great, but who is less well connected.

Incidentally, the vast majority of senior/public figures understand perfectly well that they have to receive the same treatment as everyone else. If they get stroppy then (a) they believe that everyone should be receiving better treatment (if they are right then you should improve the service to everyone) or (b) they are trying to hide something (never allow yourself to be bullied into dropping a potentially important line of questioning), or (c) they are simply pompous (in which case don't favour them, but don't set out to punish them either).

Third, it is your defence against anyone, including journalists, who might ask you to give them advice and information that you have not given to others. If possible, of course, you should be free with information. But there are no circumstances in which you should give information or advice to one person that you would not give to anyone else that asked a similar question.

Political Impartiality

This complex subject has a chapter to itself:- see chapter 3.

2.5 Appointment on Merit

The Civil Service Code says that civil servants must be appointed on merit on the basis of fair and open competition. This is what it means in practice:-

It is fairly straightforward to arrange a level transfer (i.e. without a significant pay rise) of an official from one job to another. But the need to avoid nepotism and favouritism means that you need to take great care when appointing someone from outside the civil service, or promoting someone from within it. The basic rules for these appointments are as follows.

- All such appointments must be made on the basis of fair and open competition.

- All prospective applicants must be given equal and reasonable access to adequate information about the job and its requirements, and about the selection process.

- All applicants must be considered equally on merit at each stage of the selection process.

- Selection must be based on relevant criteria applied consistently to all the candidates.

- Selection techniques must be reliable and guard against bias.

You therefore cannot appoint someone to a job without an advertisement and competition, even if you believe them to be ideally or uniquely suitable. There are limited exceptions, such as for temporary appointments and inward secondees, but you should take a close look at the relevant guidance, and consult your HR team, before attempting to make use of such exceptions.

The **Civil Service Commission's Recruitment Principles**[33] contain the latest interpretation of the basic principles discussed above.

How to Choose the Right Person

Some departments seem to think that 'fair competition' means that recruitment competitions and/or interviews should use standard questions, often delivered remotely and assessed by some computer or algorithm. This strikes me as dangerous nonsense as candidates will present with quite different strengths and weaknesses and these need to be individually explored.

Another problem is that fear of being perceived as unfair, and in particular discriminatory, means that recruiters are often reluctant to spell out exactly what attributes they **don't** want, as well as what they do want. There is, for instance, plenty of room for shy, retiring, academic individuals in some parts of the civil service, but many Whitehall and other jobs require staff to be friendly, self-starting, clear communicators and so on. These attributes need to be spelt out and appraised, or else you will end up appointing an ineffective genius - great at completing crosswords but quite incapable of making decisions or managing fellow humans with all their faults and frailties.

---

[33] https://www.civilservant.org.uk/library/2018-civil_service_commission-recruitment_principles.pdf

Much further practical advice can be found in my *Leading and Managing Policy Teams* - Part 3 of my *Senior Civil Service Survival Kit*.

2.6 Accountability

It would be easy enough for civil servants to ignore all this stuff about honesty, integrity and so on if it were not for the fact that they are accountable in some way for their behaviour. But what does 'accountability' mean, and to whom are you accountable?

What Does Accountability Mean?

Accountability means being held to account, scrutinised, and being required to give an account or explanation. It does not imply having to accept advice or instruction. Apart from through their relationship with Ministers, civil servants are not controlled by those to whom we are accountable. Indeed (with the exception of civil service lawyers', doctors' etc. professional bodies) none of the bodies to whom they are accountable can actually discipline or dismiss us. Their power is merely to criticise and to shame.

True accountability is nevertheless very powerful because it causes decision makers to think hard about the range of decisions and behaviours that are available to them, and the fairness, appropriateness and proportionality of each choice. Jonathan Haidt refers to this as *exploratory thought*, and argues (I think correctly) that effective accountability has three vital elements:

- Decision makers learn before forming any opinion that they will be accountable to an audience.

- The audience's views are unknown.

- The decision maker believes that the audience is well informed, and interested in both fairness and accuracy.

Civil servants unfortunately learn very quickly that both they and their Ministers are accountable in many different ways but (with the exception of the courts) their audiences (including Parliament) are seldom well informed and interested in both fairness and accuracy.

Accountable to Whom?

Individual civil servants are principally (and privately) responsible to Ministers who are in turn accountable to Parliament. A small number of the most senior officials are, as Accounting Officers, also directly responsible to Parliament for their stewardship of public funds.

Apart from this, however, civil servants are collectively accountable, alongside their Ministers and in a multitude of ways, for the performance of their department and its compliance with the law. Accountability is exercised in conversation and through correspondence and the media.

Accountability to Parliament

Accounting Officers are accountable direct to parliament for their, and their departments', stewardship of public funds etc. including:

- **regularity** which means the requirement for all expenditure and receipts to be dealt with in accordance with the legislation authorising them, any delegated authority and the rules of Government accounting

- **propriety** which is a further requirement that expenditure and receipts should be dealt with in accordance with Parliament's intentions and the principles of Parliamentary control, and in accordance with the values and behaviour appropriate to the public sector - see below.

- **value for money** (VFM), and

- **effective management systems**.

Parliamentary scrutiny takes place through evidence gathering by the Public Accounts Committee (the PAC) (assisted by the National Audit Office - the NAO) and other Select Committees. Accountability also occurs through Parliamentary Questions/Answers and debates, correspondence with MPs, and the Parliamentary Commissioner for Administration - the "Parliamentary Ombudsman".

But Parliamentary scrutiny unfortunately seldom meets any of Jonathan Haidt's tests listed above. Parliamentarians love 'naming and shaming', and the parliamentary spotlight too often moves frequently and unpredictably. The views of MPs, when they do get involved in one of our issues, are often highly predictable, driven by party-political considerations, and not least the governing party's need to support the Prime Minister.

Also, although Parliamentarians cannot of course be expert in many of the areas in which they are asked to form judgements, they seldom draw on sufficient, expert, outside advice. They are also not skilled in questioning those who appear before them (who - unlike MPs - often prepare for hours or days in advance of their appearance).

All this in turn means that many Parliamentary reports are politics-driven, or at least driven by a desire to look good by criticising Ministers, or criticising officials who can neither argue back nor point to bad Ministerial decision-making. It is no wonder that most PAC reports, and many Select Committee reports, have very little long term impact.

Accountability to the Public

Departmental performance and behaviour are scrutinised by the media, other interested bodies and individuals through the medium of annual reports, correspondence etc. with the public, press notices and briefings and consultation processes. These are all very important mechanisms but none of them fully meet all of Jonathan Haidt's tests.

It is occasionally useful to remember that we are not under any duty to respond to all media interest. Although we should generally aim to be free with information, there is no need to engage with media that will use their relationship with us merely for entertainment or to boost circulation.

Accountability to the Courts

Judicial Review is a very effective way of holding officials and Ministers to account; a reason, no doubt, for JR's growing popularity. Only Judicial Review meets all three of Jonathan

Haidt's tests of effective accountability, summarised above.

Audit

There is one other essential set of safeguards in the form of audit processes backed up by incorruptible management assisted by careful selection processes when senior civil servants are appointed from outside the Service. The National Audit Office, the civil service itself, and the Civil Service Commissioners, are thus themselves an integral part of the structure of accountability.

Chapter 3
Political Impartiality

The Civil Service Code says the following on the need for political impartiality:

You must:

- serve the Government, whatever its political persuasion, to the best of your ability in a way which maintains political impartiality and is in line with the requirements of this Code, no matter what your own political beliefs are;

- act in a way which deserves and retains the confidence of Ministers, while at the same time ensuring that you will be able to establish the same relationship with those whom you may be required to serve in some future Government; and

- comply with any restrictions that have been laid down on your political activities.

You must not:

- act in a way that is determined by party political considerations, or

- use official resources for party political purposes; or

- allow your personal political views to determine any advice you give or your actions.

The rest of this chapter explains what this means. Its contents are:

3.1 What does Political Impartiality Mean?

Here are the most obvious consequences:

- You may not publicly defend the decisions and views of your Ministers (as distinct from explaining them), including in the social and other media, or by writing to newspapers.

- You must even avoid saying or writing anything which could be quoted as demonstrating that you personally (or your colleagues) either agree or disagree with Ministers' decisions.

- You may not disclose the advice that you have given to Ministers. *but on the other hand:*

- You must explain and implement your Minister's policies with real commitment, whatever your personal views.

For the avoidance of doubt, you are expected to take politics into account when giving private advice to Ministers, and you are expected to help Ministers defend their policies, once they have made their decisions, even if you don't agree with them.

Here is some useful advice from experienced officials:-

Jill Rutter first:-

> 'If you can't work on a policy you disagree with, don't join the civil service! ... if you can't work on a policy you didn't vote for, then lots of other careers are available'.

Former Minister George Eustice pointed out that civil service impartiality is totally different to, for instance, the BBC's impartiality. Put bluntly, like the armed forces, the civil service supports the government, right or wrong.

Permanent Secretary Martin Donnelly, in a speech at the Institute for Government in June 2014, defined political impartiality in this way:

> [Civil servants must] not do for one Minister what would not be done for another of a different party ... in the same situation. ... Providing a convincing defence of government policy should be a core Whitehall

skill; rubbishing the Opposition is not the function of permanent officials.

I also like this *Civil Service World* summary of comments made in late 2019 by ex-Cabinet Secretary Gus O'Donnell:

> Using the example of rugby referee Nigel Owens, Lord O'Donnell made clear that "the job of the civil servant is to be impartial, but not neutral", which is an important distinction. While a referee would not "take sides", it is also "massively important that they are absolutely firm about the way the rules are conducted". In a similar vein, while civil servants "are of course politically impartial," they also "need to take sides on policy issues". "Our job is to apply honesty and objectivity to come up with clear policy recommendations," he added.

But why is this impartiality so important? According to Lord O'Donnell, there are seven key reasons:

- Impartiality allows for continuity across changes of administration.

- Impartiality is a bastion against confirmation bias.

- Impartiality builds mutual trust between civil servants and Ministers, which is vital if they are to work effectively together.

- Impartiality enables the civil service to build long-terms relationships with businesses, trade unions, the monarchy, the judiciary and other institutions.

- Many civil servants operate in delivery bodies, so if their senior personnel were to change every time there's a change of administration, it would damage their effectiveness.

- Impartiality makes the civil service a much more attractive career.

- Impartiality leads to better decisions, as it ensures Ministers are surrounded with people who are not necessarily yes men and women.

Incoming Ministers are, of course, likely to be somewhat wary of the 'continuity' argument if they want to oversee a dramatic change of policy direction. But many a novice Cabinet Minister has rued the 'brave' decisions that they took (against advice) in their first two to three months in a job. Their more experienced colleagues generally advise against replacing Permanent and Principal Private Secretaries until the Cabinet Minister has settled into the job. And (contrary to rumour) Cabinet Secretaries do not offer to resign when a new Prime Minister arrives. Their experience and familiarity with key players is initially invaluable, at least until the new PM has found their feet.

3.2 Practical Advice

It can be very hard to remain impartial, for it can make you seem quite unenthusiastic about your Minister's policies. It can be even harder when a Minister or Special Adviser does not share your view of the border between explaining and promoting a Minister's policy and party politics. As discussed in Chapter 2.3, it is particularly important that civil servants should never write or say things which they know or suspect to be untrue. If under pressure to say something which may not be true, experienced officials, including comms teams, often default to saying that 'The government [or Minister X] believes that ...' which can be followed by any old nonsense.

It can be even more difficult if you strongly support – or strongly object to – decisions that have been made, or might

be made, by Ministers. It is not always possible to hide those
views from colleagues, and it is sometimes difficult to hide
them from those outside the Government with whom you
come into frequent contact. But it is absolutely essential that
you give no sign that you oppose the principles and underlying thrust of the Government's policies, nor must you suggest
that you do not respect your Minister.

It can be tricky to follow the above advice where minor decisions are concerned. ('Of course I will try to get him to
open your conference. It's an important occasion'). But you
will learn from bitter experience that the advice is sensible,
for it is embarrassing all round when the Minister refuses to
do what you suggest. There is, I am afraid, no alternative to
sounding rather pathetic and merely promising that the case
will be put to the Minister, adding that you cannot predict the
result. Quite simply, it should never be possible for anyone
to be able to criticise Ministers for failing to take your advice. And it is even more important that incoming Ministers
should be unaware of the extent or otherwise of your personal support for their predecessors' policies.

Equally, you may not be asked to engage in activities which
call into question your political impartiality, or which give
rise to criticism that people paid from public funds are being
used for party political purposes. So:-

- You may not help draft 'Dear Colleague' letters unless they are to
  be sent to all MPs.

- You are allowed to provide Ministers with facts which might be used in political speeches etc., and you are allowed to check Ministers' political speeches for factual accuracy.

- You are also allowed to comment on the analysis, costings and proposals contained in documents produced by political organisations, including the Opposition, but you must not draft Ministers' responses to such documents.

- You may not brief an MP (including from the Government party) or agree that an MP may visit a Government office etc. without Ministerial approval. Ministers will usually agree to factual or uncontroversial briefings and visits, but they sometimes want to get involved themselves, in which case any meeting or visit has to be arranged at a time convenient for both the Minister and the MP.

Former Minister Nick Harvey offered this advice:

'One way that some submissions could be improved would be to ensure that those writing briefs stand back and think about putting their advice into a political context. Sometimes the advice strives so hard to be objective that it becomes unworldly. I was not looking for politically biased advice but I did want advice that was politically aware: political neutrality was fine, but political naivety was unhelpful.'

3.3 Is it Difficult to be Impartial?

Michael Heseltine thought that officials usually had a good sense of where the dividing line lay:

As a Minister, I found that the civil service was more than capable at making a judgement about what crossed the line of impartiality and into party political activity. There were two occasions in which a civil servant said to me "I think Secretary of State that's more Central Office than it is for us", and they were quite right and I respected that. I cannot think of any example where any corrupt proposal crossed my desk. That is quite a statement given my history. I can think of only one occasion when anyone tried to draw my attention to a party-political interest which might be benefited by a decision I was going to take. I took the opposite decision.

Rather further back in history, Claire Tomalin tells this nice tale in her biography of Samuel Pepys:

> Pepys knew perfectly well [that the war] had been badly managed, but he was bound to defend the Navy Office; and, in making the case for the defence, he was effectively defending the king and his policy also, which he had deplored in private so often. He carried out his difficult task with admirable skill. He was not required to be sincere.

Barbara Hosking, in *Exceeding My Brief*, recounts how she had been a Labour Councillor in Islington and had worked for the Labour Party in Transport House before working very closely effectively for both Labour's Harold Wilson and Conservative Ted Heath in 10 Downing Street. She also quotes the example of an ex-Army Information Officer 'who was extremely right wing, anti-union, anti-Semitic, a horror. His Minister was [hard left] Tony Benn and he worked flat out for him.'

3.4 Serial Monogamists?

Because civil servants are not totally impartial when serving the Government of the day, they are often characterised as 'serial monogamists'. Parties in government are always better served than parties out of government. The civil service advises Ministers on how best to present their policies, helps them avoid or respond to attacks, and (under the Osmotherly

Rules - see Chapter 1.4) they can provide only limited information to Select Committees.

Almost inevitably, too, civil servants become reconciled to and often supportive of policies of Governments that are in power for several years. Privatisation might have been one such policy. So there is bound to be the sound of tyres squealing if the government machine has to quickly change direction on the arrival of a new Prime Minister. It is nevertheless quite surprising how quickly officials can adapt to the quite different policies of an incoming Government, and then work very effectively to promote, defend and implement them. Many of them, indeed, enjoy the associated intellectual and practical challenges.

There is, to my mind, a bigger problem in that certain departments develop long term policy preferences which are hard to shift. The Department of Transport tends to be pro-roads; the Home Office used to have a liberal culture - but that may have disappeared; the Foreign Office likes foreigners; the Ministry of Agriculture is pro-farmer; the Department for Industry/Business generally favours intervention and manufacturing; the Department for Trade favours free trade; the Ministry of Defence loves Trident; and so on. These accusations may be unfair, but there is probably a kernel of truth in each of them. And incoming Ministers find that they, too, quickly become sympathetic to the claims and lobbying of the departments' client groups.

There also appears to be a growing problem of officials using social media to express their support for (and therefore their loyalty to) Ministers' policies. This is discussed further below.

But, as you read the rest of this chapter, try not to get excessively depressed when you encounter examples of civil servants becoming slightly too political. Here is some sensible advice from Dan Corry[34]:

> How much does the impartiality of the civil service matter in any case? I think it does matter as it ensures political policy makers get the best advice they can and should have, not advice trying to second guess what they want anyway; makes transitions from Minister to Minister and party to party much easier; and forces Ministers to at least confront information and advice that may not go with their prejudices.

> But in truth I find it hard to argue that there were key moments where this "impartiality" was crucial to the decision making I was involved in. It was most powerful where Ministers or departments were arguing over something and an honest broker was helpful. This was true for instance in the fierce arguments around the case for making the planning regime for major infrastructure projects more streamlined, where Cabinet Office held the ring well. But maybe it is good analysis and the weighing up of the options that is as important as impartiality per se. Interestingly, rational officials did not always want to head for the safe ground of pure impartiality either: sometimes they used to ask me where I thought the Secretary of State was heading as they did not want to waste hundreds of hours producing advice that was not wanted.

3.5 Political Activity

The extent to which you are allowed to be politically active depends mainly on your seniority and closeness to Ministers.

---

[34] This is an extract from Dan Corry's chapter in 'impartiality matters'. It is well worth reading the whole chapter, here:- https://www.civilservant.org.uk/library/2019-Smith_Institute-impartiality_matters.pdf.

3.5.1 Senior Officials

Senior officials such as members of the Senior Civil service, and probably also Private Office staff, are not allowed to be politically active and should not, in my view, belong to a political party, even if their membership is not public knowledge.

There have been examples of officials realising that they have developed such strong political views and/or such strong attachment to a politician boss that they cannot remain in an apolitical profession. Two that come to mind are Charles Powell who was very close to Margaret Thatcher, and Andrew Lansley who eventually became a prominent politician and Health Secretary.

I am not aware of any post-war examples of senior UK civil servants being disciplined for undertaking political activities. The simple reason is that they are almost all concentrated in London and so any such activity would immediately be detected and stopped - so nobody does it, even if they want to. In addition, of course, almost all senior officials are perfectly happy being apolitical and have no wish to undertake political activities.

There have, over the years, been a few examples of individual officials who have appeared too free with their views on policy issues and/or over enthusiastic in their defence of government policies, but not enough to suggest a serious problem. There is a more detailed commentary and list on my website[35].

---

[35] https://www.civilservant.org.uk/library/civil_servants_speaking_out.pdf

There is, however, a rather different problem in that the Johnson Government appears to have encouraged or even pressurised officials to say positive and helpful things and/or communicate misleading information. This is discussed in more detail in section 3.6 below.

3.5.2 Middle-Ranking and Junior Officials ...

... are allowed to be politically active, as long as they act with some discretion. They can join political parties, campaign locally and write to their MP, making political points, just as anyone else can. But they shouldn't refer to their employment as a civil servant.

It would be best, however, to seek departmental approval for seeking election as a District Councillor, for instance. I would expect approval to be given in most cases but an Environment Department official might (again for instance) be refused permission to seek local election on behalf of the Greens.

Here are a couple of examples of officials whose political activities were incompatible with their civil service employment:

> Dominic Shaw, a Dept for Education economist, was dismissed in 2023. It was reported that he was Secretary of the London branch of the Young Fabians and Vice President of the Young European Movement.

> UKIP politician Paula Walters was held to have been fairly dismissed in 2019 after tweeting, for instance, that she could not "tell the difference between a migrant and a terrorist". An Employment Tribunal found that "The claimant's belief that she should be able to say anything

about anyone is not worthy of respect in a democratic society. Her belief put her in inevitable conflict with the fundamental rights of others, rights protected under the Equality Act 2010".

3.5.3 Petitions

Signing a petition is unlikely to cause anyone to question your impartiality, but senior officials should be cautious. You don't want anyone to be able to point out that 'Minister X's close adviser doesn't agree with the government's policy'. I would also advise against signing a petition on a subject where you or a colleague might be asked to give policy advice. So I don't think Department of Transport officials, for instance, should sign petitions objecting to HS2.

3.6 Communications and Social Media[36]

Senior officials have a somewhat higher profile nowadays than they did in the past, particularly when they are asked to lead regulatory and other non-departmental bodies. Departments, and sometimes individual officials, are also more active on social media. Information officers, Permanent Secretaries and others consequently come under some pressure from Ministers and Spads to say positive and helpful things. This is fine, up to a point, but the rules on political impartiality still apply and it is important that they are followed.

(As an aside, the Chief Medical Officer occupies a post which is to a great extent independent of Ministers. The CMO is

---

[36] For more general advice on effective communication see https://www.civilservant.org.uk/skills-effective_communication.html

therefore allowed to indicate that they are not entirely comfortable with government policies, as Dr Chris Whitty did during the Covid pandemic.)

It is necessary to distinguish the activities of comms teams and individual media officers from comments and tweets by named officials.

Put shortly, comms teams are allowed to promote and applaud Government policies. Inconvenient facts and opposing arguments can be ignored as long as the overall message is not misleading. (And a press notice that is highly selective in its 'facts' and 'examples', or which blatantly ignores obvious questions, will anyway be seen by many as propaganda and therefore ineffective.)

It is, on the other hand, entirely inappropriate for an individual official (outside a comms team) to applaud a government policy as they might shortly be working for a Minister who had a contrary view.

Guidance for comms teams[37] is accordingly carefully drafted:-

The communication:

- should be relevant to government responsibilities

- should be objective and explanatory, not biased or polemical

- should not be – or liable to be – misrepresented as being party political

- should be conducted in an economic and appropriate way

- should be able to justify the costs as expenditure of public funds

[37] https://www.civilservant.org.uk/library/civil_servants_speaking_out.pdf

To work effectively, media officers must establish their impartiality and neutrality with the news media, and ensure that they deal with all news media even-handedly. Central to the media officer's specific role is the responsibility to help the public – by helping journalists – to understand the policies of the government of the day.

Do

- Present, describe and justify the thinking behind the policies of the Minister

- Be ready to promote the policies of the department and the Government as a whole

- Make as positive a case as the facts warrant

- Speak on the record as a departmental spokesperson wherever possible, and avoid unattributed quotes

- Insist that all political aspects are handled by the party political press office or special adviser

- Feel free to discuss any aspect of propriety with your Head of News and Director of Communications.

Don't

- Justify or defend policies in party political terms

- Expressly advance any policy as belonging to a particular political party

- Directly attack the policies and opinions of opposition parties and groups (although, on occasion, it may be necessary to respond in specific terms)

- Oversell policies, re-announce achievements or investments and claim them as new or otherwise attempt to mislead the public.

On a day-to-day basis, media officers should take particular care when handling:

- Decisions taken by Ministers fulfilling their statutory responsibilities which directly affect individuals or groups. These must be handled with particular care, to secure an impartial and objective presentation of the case that avoids inaccuracy, inconsistency or bias

- Ministerial speeches or statements

- Ministers using the Press Office to ensure that their policy and actions are explained and presented in a positive light. Ministers can do this, but care must be taken that any press activity is designed to further government objectives.

Despite this pretty clear advice, there is equally clear evidence, summarised below, that increasing abuse of official communications is a problem which needs to be addressed. The following paragraphs consider some contentious areas and examples beginning, inevitably, with ...

3.6.1 Tweets

The increasing use of Twitter/X from around 2020, and the increasingly febrile political atmosphere caused by Brexit and the COVID-19 pandemic, meant that departments' communications teams came under pressure to publish misleading information via social media, and in particular via Twitter. Each incident was minor itself but one example was a tweet in October 2020 in which the Department for International Trade claimed that a trade deal with Japan had reduced the price of soya (sic) sauce. The IfG's Alex Thomas summarised the problem very well in a blog which I repeat below. His main point, though, was that Ministers 'need the media and the public to trust what the government is saying, especially during a pandemic when effective and honest communication is the most important weapon the government has against the disease. That is not worth sacrificing for any fleeting media hit.'

Alex Thomas' Blog

The civil servant responsible for the Department for International Trade's Twitter account might in future pause before mixing baking and government messaging. As many trade experts rapidly pointed out, the department's claim on Twitter, sent out during an episode of *The Great British Bake Off*, that soy sauce "will be made cheaper thanks to our trade deal with Japan" was not accurate. The following day, DIT issued a convoluted clarification that it "will be cheaper than it otherwise would be under WTO terms, on which we would be trading with Japan from 1 Jan if we had not secured the UK-Japan trade deal".

The soya social media flurry was a trivial incident in itself, but it was the latest in a line of misleading messages from departmental twitter accounts. In August Matthew Rycroft, the permanent secretary at the Home Office, publicly accepted that the description of "activist lawyers" who were trying to "delay and disrupt returns" of migrants should not have been tweeted from the Home Office account. The Northern Ireland Office, meanwhile, continues to maintain its assertion that "there will be no border in the Irish Sea between GB & NI", convincing no-one of anything except an ability to dance on semantic pinheads, and despite officials on both sides of the Irish Sea working hard to implement an array of the checks necessary to cross what becomes a trade border between GB and the EU.

This increasing abuse of official communications is a problem which needs to be addressed.

Civil service and special adviser codes require honest communication

These accounts are funded by the taxpayer for the purpose of informing the public – not misleading them. The civil service code requires civil servants to "set out the facts and relevant issues truthfully" and not to "deceive or knowingly mislead Ministers, Parliament or others" – and that applies to their special adviser colleagues as well. The professional standards for communications specialists are even more explicit, requiring messages to be "objective and explanatory, not biased or polemical". If government cannot meet these standards when trying to do fast paced communication, it needs to hold off, not lower the standards.

It is the art of government press officers to simplify complex policies and concepts into material that is more easily accessed by the media and public. There is no bar to those messages presenting the government's plans positively, indeed a lot of effort goes into finding the best way of presenting material to put the government in the best light. But there is a world of difference between a legitimate gloss and deliberately misleading the public. Communications directors and their permanent secretaries need to police that boundary in all our interests.

Government needs to ensure its sign off processes prevent misleading messages

Formal public government statements or quotes are almost always written by committee, with at least three contributors: a policy expert, a press officer and a Minister (or more often a special adviser delegated to act on the Minister's behalf). In general, the more controversial or novel the issue, the more senior the clearance required. This can be clunky and results in frantic late night email chains when an unexpected story breaks, but it gives the government a good chance to ensure that messages are accurate, intelligible and in line with its political and wider policy approach.

Something seems to be going wrong with this protocol. Perhaps it is the speed of social media and the desire of civil service communications teams to be pacy, informal and relevant that means checks are getting missed. Or perhaps it is a more conscious attempt by Ministers and their advisers to test the boundaries, stir up controversies and turn official government outlets into campaigning tools.

Either way, it is permanent secretaries, as the most senior civil servants in their departments and the guardians of their teams' propriety and ethics standards, who need to enforce a sign off process, even for seemingly innocuous tweets about condiments.

Government will be less effective if it is seen as serially untrustworthy

This government has decided to centralise its communications. In theory this is a perfect opportunity to enforce a streamlined but authoritative accuracy and propriety check. More likely it will mean official messaging being further removed from the policy experts, and nearer to a No.10 communications operation that has not stood out for its reverence for the facts.

It is in Ministers' own interest to act to keep this tendency in check. They need the media and the public to trust what the government is saying, especially during a pandemic when effective and honest communication is the most important weapon the government has against the disease. That is not worth sacrificing for any fleeting media hit.

Here are some other examples of problem tweets:

The Foreign Office Twitter feed said this in January 2022:

'The Northern Ireland Protocol was designed to protect the peace process and respect all communities in Northern Ireland. It is doing the opposite."

This may have been a quote from a speech by Foreign Secretary Liz Truss in which case this should have been made clear. Without such an explanation, I think that this tweet was on the wrong side of the line.

Even more blatantly, Prime Minister Johnson's official Twitter feed, reporting on a visit to Batley, urged readers to vote for Conservative candidate Ryan Stephenson in a forthcoming elections. This was so wrong that I fail to see how it got published. Equally, I was surprised to see the same Twitter account on 11 February 2022 celebrating the anniversary of Mrs Thatcher's election as leader of the Conservative Party (#IronLady !). In fairness, however, the vast majority of the Johnson tweets fell within the boundary of what is allowed.

Senior officials, too, are sometimes too keen to suck up to Ministers. One Head of the Civil Service & Cabinet Secretary sent out tweets drawing attention to 'good news' such as low unemployment rates, "tough new measures to tackle tax avoidance, evasion and non-compliance" and the:

> "historic visit of Saudi Crown Prince Mohammed bin Salman to UK which secures $100bn of long term mutual investment, drawing on UK world leading expertise in health, education, finance."

If there was any bad news, it didn't feature in his Twitter feed, and his media activity would surely have made for some 'interesting' conversations with a new Prime Minister.

Here is a slightly different example from the same source:

> "Great speech from Matt Hancock on building a smarter, nimbler more responsive & accessible state"

What a nice thing to say! The Minister - Matt Hancock - was, after all, talking about building a better government machine and could reasonably expect officials to welcome it. But what if his speech had included plans which the Cabinet Secretary had previously opposed? Would he have declined to issue supportive comment, and would the absence of such comment draw attention to the rift between Minister and officials? It would be better, I think, to issue factual press releases summarising what Ministers are aiming to achieve, rather than expect senior officials to praise every Ministerial pronouncement or - even worse - just some of them.

3.6.2 Official Photographs

Several Ministers, beginning with Prime Minister Cameron and including several in the Johnson government (including Mr Johnson himself, Chancellor Rishi Sunak and Foreign Secretary Liz Truss) persuaded their officials to employ 'vanity snappers' on the public payroll. More than 700 photos of Ms Truss had been uploaded to the Government's official account on photo-sharing platform Flickr during her first five months as Foreign Secretary. It was also reported that the MoD arranged for one of their planes to fly a 1200km round trip to take part in a Prime Ministerial photoshoot. These costs are clearly expended for no reason other than to boost Ministers' images so it seems doubtful that this is an appropriate use of public funds, though I have yet to see a formal challenge. I also agree with Francis Elliott who noted that "what is really damaging is the extent to which the official government picture is displacing an independent record".

3.6.3 Embargos

It is often sensible to let reputable journalists read complex announcements before they are made available to the wider public - but not if the decision is market sensitive.

'No approach' embargoes - which forbid journalists to talk to those who have also seen the document and might have views - are seldom necessary. Newspapers have anyway been known to ignore the 'no approach' embargo, where it is clearly inappropriate.

It is also OK for media officers to help Ministers pre-brief the media in advance of the publication of significant and controversial reports etc. Again though, the briefing should not be so one-sided as to be misleading. And we are entitled to expect decent journalists and others to look beyond Ministers' 'lines to take' and form their own conclusions.

3.7 Prime Minister's Office

Some, but not all, of the above rules do rather break down under the intense pressure experienced by those working in No.10 Downing Street. Senior staff in the Prime Minister's office need to tread a fine line between serving the Prime Minister and remaining remote from the business of party leader. Private Secretaries, Press Secretaries and others inevitably have to take strong lines when communicating both inside and outside Whitehall so as to ensure that the PM's political priorities are firmly embedded in everything they say and do. This includes drafting speeches and press notices.

Here is Dan Corry's analysis[38]:

> Things work rather differently in Downing Street. There is much closer working between officials and political appointees than in the departments. Things move too fast for people to stand on ceremony, or for officials to feel uncomfortable that politics is happening all the time. There are also more than the usual two SPADs, so there is as much tension between the political appointees as between them and the civil service. In some ways, I felt that all at No 10 were united in being "against" OGDs (other government departments) who never went fast enough, put up pointless excuses, and cared more about their departmental interests than of the government as a whole. This is all hard for civil servants in No 10, who need to keep their independence as well, advising the PM – and the powerful SPADs – of what the evidence says, and trying to keep as much as possible to the proper way of going about things, consulting the relevant departments and so on.

Former Cabinet Secretary Robin Butler was quite candid, when briefing his biographer, about his deep involvement in writing speeches for Mrs Thatcher when he was her Principal Private Secretary. He even wrote in a personal capacity, offering her handling advice during the Westland crisis, after he had returned to the Treasury. But he didn't go so far as Charles Powell, another Private Secretary, who became far too closely associated with Mrs Thatcher and eventually could not (and did not want to) return to his civil service career.

On the other hand *The Guardian* once 'revealed' that Press Secretary and civil servant Bernard Ingham had advised Conservative Prime Minister Margaret Thatcher that her first media priority was to "look after the Daily Mail"-

---

[38] This is an extract from Dan Corry's chapter in 'impartiality matters'. It is well worth reading the whole chapter, here:- https://www.civilservant.org.uk/library/2019-Smith_Institute-impartiality_matters.pdf.

despite (the Guardian said) neutrality rules that banned him from doing so. The Guardian was wrong. (Later) Sir Bernard had in fact given perfectly sensible private advice and would have given similar advice to a Labour Minister - although probably mentioning another paper.

Bernard Ingham in fact had strong Labour roots but nevertheless pleaded "utterly, completely and wholeheartedly guilty" to the charge of news management on behalf of Mrs Thatcher. He sought to co-ordinate ministerial pronouncements and flag up important papers, and lunched with journalists almost daily. His job, he said, was to promote government policy to the very best of his ability. He never attended a Conservative party conference, or knowingly visited Thatcher's constituency of Finchley in north London, but he trod a delicate path. As he wrote in his memoirs: "It was this burning love of her country and her manifest determination to restore its fortunes that inspired me. She needed all the help and support she could get if she were to have a fighting chance of achieving half of what she hoped for Britain. It was my duty as a civil servant to give her that full-hearted support. I have never had much time for those civil servants who argue that their proper duty is to withhold that last ounce from the elected government lest they become over-committed."

3.8 General Elections and National Referendums

The term '*purdah*' is often used, unofficially, to describe the period immediately after the dissolution of Parliament and before an election or referendum when there are additional restrictions on the activity of civil servants. More literally, it is also called the 'pre-election period'. The term comes from the Urdu and Persian words for veil or curtain, also used to describe the practice of screening women from men or strangers. Its English usage accordingly suggests Whitehall drawing a veil over itself and cutting itself off, as far as possible, from the electorate.

Here are the basic rules:

Unless it runs for the full extent of a fixed term, Parliament is usually dissolved two or three days after the Prime Minister announces the date of the election. If the Opposition agrees, this allows the completion of important legislation, such as Finance Bills.

MPs cease to be MPs when Parliament is dissolved. Strictly speaking, therefore, all candidates are thereafter on an equal footing. But it is regarded as courteous for Ministers themselves to reply to letters written by MPs before the dissolution, or by former MPs after the dissolution. Private Secretary replies are normally sent to candidates (Government or Opposition) who were not members before the dissolution.

Ministers retain their appointments until the Prime Minister is ready to begin to appoint the next Government.

During the pre-election period, the Government retains its responsibility to govern and Ministers remain in charge of their departments. Essential business must be carried on, but it is customary for Ministers to observe discretion as to initiating any new action of a continuing or long-term nature.

Civil servants are allowed to provide Ministers with facts which might be used in political speeches etc., and are allowed to check Ministers' political speeches for factual accuracy. They are also allowed to comment on the analysis, costings and proposals contained in documents produced by political organisations, including the Opposition, but must not draft Ministers' responses to such documents.

Ministers usually try to avoid official engagements because they want to devote the time to campaigning. But they are free to undertake engagements they regard as important, although they should seek to avoid giving the impression that they are using such occasions for party political purposes. Similarly, attendance at some international meetings remains necessary. However, before undertaking to fulfil international commitments, Ministers should consider whether the subject matter is such that they can speak with the authority proper to a representative of Her Majesty's Government.

So far as the handling of correspondence is concerned, the general rule is that citizens' individual interests should not be prejudiced by the calling of an election. It follows that letters relating to them should be replied to, whether by Ministers or by officials on their behalf. But remember that correspondence may become public and might be used for political purposes. Replies to letters should therefore be as straightforward as possible, should avoid controversy, and, if to a candidate, should not distinguish between candidates of different parties.

All public appointments which might be regarded as politically sensitive should be frozen until after the election and, although routine information activities (i.e. the provision of factual information) continue during the election campaign, other information activities generally cease entirely.

Further detail is in the relevant chapter of The Cabinet Manual[39] and in detailed guidance issued by the Cabinet Office at the beginning of the pre-election period.

The guidance issued by the Cabinet Secretary before the 2016 EU Referendum is on my website[40]. Note, however, that he made it clear (when being interrogated by the (largely Eurosceptic) Public Administration Select Committee) that civil servants would continue to provide easily available factual material for all Ministers, even if such facts might be used by pro-Brexit Ministers to attack the Government's position. But civil servants would not go further and provide briefing and speech material that supported the 'Out' position.

---

[39] https://www.civilservant.org.uk/library/2011_cabinet-manual.pdf
[40] https://www.civilservant.org.uk/library/2016_EU_Referendum_Guidance.pdf

3.9 Further Reading

The Smith Institute has published an interesting collection of essays: *impartiality matters: perspectives on the importance of impartiality in the civil service in a "post truth" world*[41].

And it is interesting (and entertaining) to read Cabinet Secretary Robert Armstrong's note of the events following the election of a hung parliament in March 1974. This election led to the resignation of Ted Heath's government and the appointment of Harold Wilson as Prime Minister. The document is on the website of the *Margaret Thatcher Foundation*[42].

---

[41] https://www.civilservant.org.uk/library/2019-Smith_Institute-impartiality_matters.pdf
[42] http://fc95d419f4478b3b6e5f-3f71d0fe2b653c4f00f32175760e96e7.r87.cf1.rackcdn.com/E39D78DE7FBF4C7583FDFC8F7A029D42.pdf

Chapter 4
No! Minister

This chapter discusses what might or should happen if civil servants have grave concerns about what Ministers are asking them to do. Broadly in order of increasing seriousness, it addresses these questions:-

What should you do if ...

4.1. ... a Minister rejects your advice?
4.2. ... a Minister requires you to implement a policy with which you profoundly disagree?
4.3. ... a Minister will not provide adequate resources?
4.4. ... a Minister asks you to do something illegal or improper?
4.5. ... you believe that a previously legitimate government is developing clear authoritarian tendencies?
4.6. The Effectiveness Trap: Can an unhappy official achieve more by leaving - or by staying and seeking to improve things from within?

4.1 What should you do if a Minister rejects your advice?

Ministers will sometimes, for their own reasons, indicate that they intend to take a decision which, although legally allowed, is not in accordance with your advice. How hard should you push back?

In most cases – you do nothing. There are lots of decisions which are close calls and do not need to be challenged

Other decisions are inevitably and properly influenced by Minsters' political beliefs. Officials cannot be expected to lose sleep if they are asked to implement policies with which they strongly disagree and/or which reverse the policies endorsed by previous Ministers. (See Paul Johnson's essay on fairness[43] if you are not already aware of how perfectly decent people can have diametrically opposed views of what is 'fair".) And then, as one official rather sarcastically remarked: Sometimes you have to let Ministers find out for themselves that an un-negotiable position is ..er.. unnegotiable.

This extract from a 1983 Reith Lecture[44] is the classic statement of your duty.

> Now, a good official will not normally take a single apparently perverse decision by his Minister as the final word: he will seek to bring him round to his own way of thinking. Indeed, if his professional conscience drives him to argue for a course of action – within the framework set by Ministers – he believes to be right, it is positively his duty to face any unpopularity he may be courting.

[43] https://www.civilservant.org.uk/library/2018-Paul_Johnson-fairness.pdf
[44] https://www.civilservant.org.uk/library/1983_reith3.pdf

A wise Minister will respect an official who does this, and realise that an apparently tiresome adviser may be the best safeguard against his own folly. .... But if he fails to persuade his Minister on a particular issue, what should a civil servant do? As our system operates, his duty is to accept, as phlegmatically as possible, the verdict of the publicly accountable Minister.

My own less elegant advice is as follows:

First, your boss and your colleagues need to be told about your concerns. They will help you decide whether to try to change the Minister's mind, and should support you if you decide to try to do so. If time is short, you may need to bring in the 'big guns'.

Barbara Hosking, author of *Exceeding My Brief*, tells a nice story of when she was a duty press officer in the Department of the Environment over a weekend in the middle of the 1976 drought. There were strict nation-wide laws restricting the use of water for many non-essential purposes, but she picked up that officials intended to press on with Monday's scheduled and legally-permitted washing of the windows of a large office block in central London. She tried to persuade the Permanent Secretary that this would be a PR nightmare (as well as wrong) but he argued that there was a contract in place and then put the phone down on her. Her only option - other than to let the story unfold - was to call Robert Armstrong, the Cabinet Secretary, and get him to ring the stupid Perm Sec. The details of the conversation were not recorded ... but the window cleaning did not take place.

If a Minister makes a decision that you and your colleagues consider to be seriously wrong then you have the right – indeed it is your responsibility – to check (a) that the Minister has been presented in writing with all the relevant facts and arguments, and with a clear recommendation, in a form which he can easily assimilate, and (b) that he or she has read the advice and has understood all the important factors. If this has not happened then you should consult the Minister's Private Secretary about the best way to correct matters.

> Why written advice? Important decisions must never be based merely on oral briefing, or on a PowerPoint presentation. This is to ensure that such decisions are soundly based on proper consideration of all the relevant facts and arguments, clearly laid out in a logical way.

If you feel that the Minister needs to think again then further written advice will often be enough, including any necessary apology for failing to prepare comprehensive advice the first time round. But if comprehensive advice has already been submitted, and the decision is important enough, then you should press for the opportunity to argue the case a second time, preferably in person. If the Minister then still rejects your recommendation then you must accept the decision. It is not for you to question the political or strategic thinking that might have contributed to the decision in question unless, exceptionally, the Minister appears to be ignoring legal advice or defying Government policy, e.g. by failing to consult interested colleagues.

You should throughout keep careful records. If it all goes pear-shaped, you need to be able to demonstrate, after the event, that you did speak truth to power[45] but were not heeded. Hopefully, you will never need to use your record but writing it will help you relax and get over it.

---

[45] https://www.civilservant.org.uk/richborne_publishing.html#STtP

4.2 What should you do if a Minister requires you to implement a policy with which you profoundly disagree?

The short answer is 'nothing'. Civil servants are duty bound to obey those who have been properly elected to form a government. Who are we to judge whether a policy is truly dreadful, when it has been properly publicised and appears to be supported by a majority of Parliamentarians? This is even more true when a policy has been included in the manifesto on which a new government has been elected. Officials should point out any negative and other unintended consequences of a manifesto policy, but their principal responsibility is to help Ministers fulfil the promises on which they were elected.

The classic statement is again to be found in that 1983 Reith lecture. Note in particular that 'the civil service cannot be thought of as an in-built safeguard against what some people might call the excesses of a radical or reforming government'.

> ... what is a career civil servant to do if he finds himself having to implement a policy with which he may strongly disagree? As I have already said, his professional code requires him to carry out his instructions with complete loyalty. But how enthusiastically and how energetically should he be expected to do this? Enthusiasm may be asking rather a lot, but I have my doubts in any case about its place in administration: it can colour judgment and lead to unwise decisions. Even the politically committed should be wary of enthusiasm. But energy is a different matter. This is a question of conscience, and of dedication to the professional

ethic. The energetic pursuit of Ministerial objectives is something that must be required of officials. And this obligation on civil servants transcends by far any qualms they may feel about the rightness of policy.

Pushed to extremes, of course, this sounds like the philosophy of Eichmann and of the German officials who loyally carried out the orders of the Hitler regime on the grounds that it was not their business to challenge government policy. I do not, however, accept the parallel. Notwithstanding the loyalty of a civil servant to the government, his conscience should clearly require him to oppose actions which are either unlawful, unconstitutional, or which involve some great affront to human values. In the last analysis he must be prepared to resign his appointment. But in such circumstances, I believe, he should be relieved of his normal obligation to refrain from commenting on policies for which he may have drafted official advice.

But all this is to describe an exceptional situation. What the basic doctrine means, and it is important to understand this, is that the Civil Service cannot be thought of as an in-built safeguard against what some people might call the excesses of a radical or reforming government. The only effective safeguards, if it is safeguards we are seeking, have to be found in the political and judicial processes, or in the force of circumstances themselves – and let me say parenthetically that I have usually found that force of circumstances Is the most effective safeguard of the three.

The Armstrong Memorandum[46], first published two years later, codifies the above as follows:

When, having been given all the relevant information and advice, the Minister has taken a decision, it is the duty of civil servants loyally to carry out that decision with precisely the same energy and good will, whether they agree with it or not.

---

[46] See Chapter 1.3 for more detail

The Windrush crisis was perhaps a good example of officials carrying out a policy about which they had serious concerns. It arose because duly elected Ministers mandated a deliberately 'hostile environment' for undocumented immigrants. Home Office policy officials were not the only ones who warned that this would lead to severe and unwarranted hardship for undocumented British citizens. But it was for HM Opposition in Parliament, the media, and maybe the courts, to challenge the policy if they felt it was wrong - and it is to the credit of the media that they eventually did so. The system worked, eventually, without civil servants appearing to turn on the Prime Minister and Home Secretary. As Adam Wagner correctly surmised:

> 'People will forget this scandal, and nobody will resign from their jobs. Why should they? They were doing their jobs. The hostile environment was never a secret. The system will remain unfair unless we [the public] fundamentally rethink our approach to migration.

But it is well recognised[47] that, if a decision offends a civil servant's personal conscience, they have the right to ask to be moved to different work or, ultimately, to leave the civil service.

And some do indeed resign. I return to this subject towards the end of this chapter but here are some examples:

Richard Haviland resigned in 2019. He then released his resignation letter which stressed that his decision was 'based not on Brexit, but on what has ensued from it [including

---

[47] Confirmed by a former Cabinet Secretary in a letter to The Times on 4 July 2019

Theresa May's] refusal to be honest with the British population about the implications of [her post-referendum policy] choices'.

Alexandra Hall Hall resigned from the Foreign Office because she felt that she was asked to lie about the likely consequences of the UK leaving the EU Single Market and Customs Union. Her 'internal struggle' will resonate with every public servant that has considered resigning because they are unhappy with what they are being asked to do. In it she draws a helpful distinction between resigning because you do not agree with a policy, and resigning because you believe that a policy is unethical or even illegal.

> 'My resignation came after many months of internal struggle. As I agonized over my decision, I grappled with many of the same dilemmas that have faced other public servants, in both the United States and the United Kingdom, when tasked with implementing a policy with which they do not agree, or that they consider unethical or even illegal. Is our primary duty to the elected government of the day, even when it may be breaking the law or wilfully deceiving the public? Or is our duty to some broader notion of the "public good"? If the latter, how is that to be defined, and by whom?

> If we stay silent in the face of wrongdoing, do we become complicit ourselves? But if we speak out, are we breaking our pledge of impartial service to the government of the day and undermining the foundation of trust between politicians and officials? If we resign, do we let down our colleagues and institutions? Do we merely allow others with fewer scruples to fill our shoes? But if we stay on, are we knowingly violating our duty to provide ethical public service to our fellow citizens?'

Personal circumstances will affect individual decisions, of course. Age, available savings and re-employment prospects may all be relevant.

In most cases, however, the resignation decision is taken out of individuals hands. Dissenters will typically begin by politely refusing to acquiesce in dubious policy decisions, and/or gently challenging what they are being asked to do. But their dissent will be noted and – unless strongly backed by their bosses – their 'corridor reputation' and hence promotability will be negatively impacted. They will – rather sooner than later – find themselves in jobs where they are no longer (in the view of their Permanent Secretary) rubbing Ministers up the wrong way. And if they are themselves Permanent Secretaries they will find themselves out of a job – accompanied by a good deal of taxpayers' cash, as happened to quite a few of them following Prime Minister Johnson's appointment.

It is rather harder to sideline or dismiss someone who questions the very legality of a government policy. Carne Ross resigned from the British Foreign and Commonwealth Office in 2004 after giving (then-secret) evidence to the Butler Inquiry — a review set up by the British government to examine the intelligence on Iraq's weapons of mass destruction. He had concerns about the legality of the basis for war, that the case for war was being exaggerated, and that no serious effort was being made to explore alternatives to war.

Elizabeth Wilmshurst, former deputy legal adviser in the Foreign and Commonwealth Office, threatened to resign over Iraq, in March 2003. Here is her resignation letter:

1. I regret that I cannot agree that it is lawful to use force against Iraq without a second Security Council resolution to revive the authorisation given in SCR 678. I do not need to set out my reasoning; you are aware of it. My views accord with the advice that has been given consistently in this office before and after the adoption of UN security council resolution 1441 and with what the attorney general gave us to understand was his view prior to his letter of 7 March. (The view expressed in that letter has of course changed again into what is now the official line.) I cannot in conscience go along with advice - within the Office or to the public or Parliament - which asserts the legitimacy of military action without such a resolution, particularly since an unlawful use of force on such a scale amounts to the crime of aggression; nor can I agree with such action in circumstances which are so detrimental to the international order and the rule of law.

2. I therefore need to leave the Office: my views on the legitimacy of the action in Iraq would not make it possible for me to continue my role as a Deputy Legal Adviser or my work more generally. For example in the context of the International Criminal Court, negotiations on the crime of aggression begin again this year. I am therefore discussing with Alan Charlton whether I may take approved early retirement. In case that is not possible this letter should be taken as constituting notice of my resignation.

3. I joined the Office in 1974. It has been a privilege to work here. I leave with very great sadness.

(Although she made clear her readiness to resign, Wilmshurst sought and was eventually approved to take early retirement instead.)

As well as lawyers, UK Diplomats and overseas development officials seem to hate being asked to talk nonsense or tell lies

– at least when the lies are easily exposed. The dismissal of UKRep's Ivan Rogers, for speaking truth to Prime Minister Theresa May, is another example, as was the 2021 resignation of Alexandra Hall Hall. Here are some further extracts from her account of it:

> ...for most of my time as a British diplomat, I felt proud about how our system functioned ... [but] ... when I was asked to brief American businesses with significant investments in the United Kingdom, I found myself struggling to maintain the line that there would be no harmful consequences for them, even if the United Kingdom left the European Union without any deal at all. I found it hard to brush aside the concerns of congressional aides working for members of the Irish-American caucus. Sometimes I had no answers to the questions that U.S. stakeholders posed to me. The internal dissonance became acute: The professional ethos of the British Diplomatic Service was that we were upstanding civil servants, steeped in integrity, who never told lies. And yet, that was precisely what I was being asked to do.

> But when I relayed back to London that the talking points needed changing, or tried to persuade British Ministers passing through Washington of the need for more compelling arguments, I had little success. A few officials in London agreed with me, and for a while we chipped away to tighten the points here and there. But eventually we reached the limit of what could be achieved. Colleagues told me that the prevailing atmosphere in Whitehall meant that all civil servants had to be "on message," and that any points which did not comport with Ministers' preconceived notions were simply rejected. One colleague working on Northern Ireland was nearly in tears as he told me how he simply could not get his Minister to register the enormous damage that would be done to the fabric of Northern Ireland, politically and economically, if the United Kingdom left the European Union without a deal. A low point for me was when I heard a senior British Minister openly and

offensively, in front of a U.S. audience, dismiss the impact of a "No Deal" Brexit on Irish businesses as just affecting "a few farmers with turnips in the back of their trucks."

With the public messages still containing several egregious distortions, in September 2019 I decided to submit a formal complaint to the Foreign and Commonwealth Office, identifying the specific points where I felt they had violated the civil service code of integrity and political impartiality. This had a stronger effect: I received a reply a few weeks later, telling me that the process for approving the talking points had been changed, to ensure that a career civil servant, not a political adviser, was the last person to sign off on them before they were distributed to embassies.

But although this resulted in the official talking points improving a bit, it did not stop the Prime Minister and other members of his cabinet from continuing to use the old lines, with their distortions and inaccuracies. When I briefed American audiences using the new messages, the first question would always be why the prime Minister was saying something different, to which there was no easy comeback. What I was saying was not convincing to me, and no matter how I spun it, it was not convincing to my audiences. But, in the end, my decision to leave was more personal. The internal conflict over what I was being asked to do simply became unbearable.

4.3 What should you do if a Minister will not provide adequate resources?

Ministers are frequently accused of being too ready to seek political advantage by announcing impossible or badly thought-through policy objectives, or by allocating insufficient time and resources to otherwise achievable policy objectives. Jill Rutter's half jest summarised the underlying issues rather well:

> Civil servants say to Ministers that "We won't tell you it can't be done if you won't sack us when it is not done". Maybe it is time we recognised that this constitutional pact has run out of road?

Select Committees and others have responded by recommending that it should be made easier for senior civil servants to challenge Ministers' policy decisions in the same way as they have for many years been able to challenge a Ministerial spending decision. (Officials can already ask for a formal written 'Direction' if Ministers want to spend public money sin a way that appears to be irregular, or improper, or to represent poor value for money.) Further information about these developments is in chapter 6. The following paragraphs consider the recent controversies, before these developments have bedded in.

Austerity

The austerity policies of PMs David Cameron and his successors caused difficulties for all officials who were leading front line public sector organisations. What were they to say and do, internally and externally?

First, of course, they were under a profound duty to speak truth to power and to be very clear about the consequences of budget cuts. Their warnings should have drawn attention to the likelihood of life-changing consequences such as more frequent accidents, violence and deaths.

There were for instance six Justice Secretaries between 2009 and 2017 who between them required Prison Service staffing to fall by 25%. One has to hope that they were clearly warned that prisons there would be many more assaults on staff (they doubled over that period) and many more prisoner suicides. (Total deaths in custody rose from 169 in 2009 to 354 in 2016, including 104 and 206 suicides respectively.)

It will also be interesting to read, in due course, whether Department of Health officials required their Ministers to acknowledge the risks involved in running down pre-Covid pandemic precautions, and whether DCLG Ministers were aware of the risks taken by their department and agencies that probably helped cause the Grenfell Tower fire.

But what should senior managers in delivery organisations say to their staff and their external 'customers', if that is the right word? Permanent Secretaries and their policy-making colleagues can remain anonymous but those in other leadership positions cannot. There have been particularly stark problems in the criminal justice system.

Criminal Justice

Durham Chief Constable Mike Barton set an excellent example when he said that ...

> "You can hold me to account on the quality and the efficiency with which we do our work. But you can't hold me to account on the resources that we have. That is decided by others.... There has been a 30% real term cut in police resources since 2010."

But others were less honest.

Richard Foster, the retiring Head of the Criminal Cases Review Commission, was challenged on the Today Programme in October 2018 by Liam Allan, a young man whose life had been nearly destroyed by police service mistakes. The CCRC, it transpired, was now working with only 30-40% of resources that had previously been made available to it but - according to Mr Foster - its performance was just fine. Mr Allan was not persuaded.:

> "... now is the time for everyone to turn round and say " You know what, we'll hold our hands up ... we aren't at the place we all want to be" ... [It would set an] example [for others in the system] if the CCRC [were] willing to accept that it is under resourced and can't to the inquiries properly".

Susan Acland-Hood (the Chief Executive of *the Courts and Tribunal Service*) and Alison Saunders (the Director of Public Prosecutions (DPP)) were later criticised for acquiescing in and defending or down-playing staff and budget cuts. Cuts in legal aid exacerbated the problems. The result was well documented in the media and also in *the Secret Barrister's 'Stories of the Law and How it is Broken'*. By way of contrast, Ms Saunders' successor, Max Hill, warned the Commons Justice Committee, only a few weeks after his appointment, that the Crown Prosecution Service could "absolutely not" take any more staff cuts, having already lost 30% of its staff over the previous five years.

It was, to many, particularly galling that DPP Alison Saunders' gave an interview shortly before she retired in which she said that her organisation and the police were critically short

of the skills and resources required to combat crime. The
Secret Barrister responded:

> "Gosh. If only this Alison Saunders, talking honestly about the chron-
> ic under-resourcing of the Crown Prosecution Service, had been DPP.
> Instead for 5 years we've had that obliging civil servant blithely insisting
> that all was well as the CPS burned."

I chipped in, via Twitter, with the standard line that civil servants may not publicly attack Ministers' resourcing decisions
and this generated some interesting further comments and
questions.

- The Secret Barrister pointed out that "Alison Saunders went out
  of her way to pretend that there were no problems. That was the
  issue that really grated."

- Michael Heery pointed out that officials in the health sector had
  gone much farther than the DPP in talking about the effect of cuts.

- AJP Wood asked "Surely civil servants already aren't allowed to
  be anything other than honest per the Civil Service Code?:- [civil
  servants] must not deceive or knowingly mislead Ministers, Parliament or others."

- And ex-Home Office Lorraine Rogerson noted that budget cuts
  undermined the constitutional independence of the DPP who
  needed to maintain the support of the criminal bar and the police.

Where does all this leave us?

It seems to me that civil servants such Ms Acland-Hood
and Ms Saunders acted constitutionally correctly in declining even to express mild concern about the consequences of
Ministers' resourcing decisions. They cannot be as free as
those running the health service (who are not civil servants)

nor as free as those civil servants running non-Ministerial government departments[49] such as some of the regulators.

However ... as AJP Wood pointed out, senior officials have an overring duty (under the Civil Service Code) to be honest [50]. If they don't feel able to tell the whole truth, they should keep quiet and make it clear that they are doing so at the request of Ministers. They should not write or speak in a way that suggests that all is well with their organisation when it is clear that there are problems.

And we do not have to continue to accept the current constitutional position. Dissenting voices, challenge, and creative tension should all be welcomed and indeed promoted if good services with integrity are to be delivered and improved. This point was made with some force by the Chair of the Public Accounts Committee, speaking to *the Times* in June 2018:

> Britain should change a "crazy" system that stops Ministry of Defence officials from publicly voicing concerns about the armed forces budget for fear of harming their careers, a senior MP has said. Meg Hillier, chairwoman of the Public Accounts Committee, expressed her frustration at hearing evidence from several permanent secretaries and military chiefs who failed to reveal the extent of a funding hole in the MoD's plans.

> "I rail against the system which gets civil servants in front of us unable to say something that they would say is against government policy," Ms Hillier, who has served on the committee for seven years, told *The Times*. Accounting officers should be telling us there is a real challenge here in the budget. You don't get that enough. I think that there is a very big concern about how a civil servant can't say 'We can't afford this, we are

---

[49] https://www.civilservant.org.uk/information-definitions.html
[50] See Chapter 2.3.

going to have to cut something'. They would stray into what they would say is political territory and policy decisions, and they are not allowed to do that because that is what the Ministers do. It is a crazy system."

I return to this question in Chapter 6.

4.4 What should you do if a Minister asks you to do something illegal or improper?

Ministers are in practice very unlikely to ask officials to do something illegal - or 'improper' as (narrowly) defined by the Treasury and the Public Accounts Committee[51]. On the rare occasions that they do so, colleagues, including both senior Ministers and senior officials, will usually strongly resist such requests. You should certainly not comply with such a request, and you should immediately alert more senior colleagues, probably including your department's legal adviser.

It is telling that I can think of very few examples of such behaviour, but here are some possible examples:

Suez

Following the 1956 Suez Crisis, Cabinet Secretary Sir Norman Brook failed to prevent Sir Anthony Eden from lying to the House of Commons ('there was not foreknowledge that Israel would attack Egypt'), He then obeyed the PM's instruction to destroy documents, including the Sèvres protocol, which confirmed the collusion between Britain, France and Israel.

---

[51] 'Propriety is the further requirement that expenditure and receipts should be dealt with in accordance with Parliament's intentions and the principles of Parliamentary control, including the conventions agreed with Parliament.' https://www.civilservant.org.uk/library/2004_Regularity_Propriety_VFM.pdf - Chapter 5

I doubt that any modern Cabinet Secretary would accept such an order, not least because of the likelihood of his/her behaviour being exposed. But they would have to think hard about what to do if a Prime Minister were to lie to Parliament. If the lie had been inadvertent, they would need to make sure that the PM was aware of this so that it could if necessary be corrected. If the PM were reluctant to correct a lie then a Cabinet Secretary would need to decide whether it was in the clear national interest to expose the lie, depending very much on whether it might have serious consequences.

'Spycatcher'

The 1987 book *Spycatcher*, by ex-MI5 officer Peter Wright, made explosive claims about the UK's espionage operations. The government tried to stop its publication, including in Australia where Cabinet Secretary Robert Armstrong was forced to reveal in court that he had been 'economical with the truth' when he signed a letter that was deliberately misleading.

But a more serious issue was revealed when previously secret documents were declassified in December 2023. According to the *Financial Times*, Robert Armstrong also told the Australian court that it was totally untrue that he had in 1980 helped journalist Chapman Pincher write a sympathetic article about MI5 Chief Roger Hollis who was, for a time, suspected of being a Soviet agent. (Peter Wright's book contained a section about Hollis.) The papers published in 2023 revealed that this was a pure lie.

As with Suez (see above) I hope that no modern Cabinet Secretary would lie to a court, whether in the UK or overseas, not least because of the likelihood of their behaviour being exposed.

Export Guarantees

There was one occasion - many years ago - when a trade minister and his officials were very keen to offer a government backed guarantee to facilitate a major export to a purchaser who was assessed as having a high risk of defaulting when it came to paying for the goods. The guarantee needed Treasury approval which was not forthcoming so, as a Friday evening deadline approached, the Minister ordered his officials to issue the guarantee anyway, which they did. Treasury Ministers were not amused and the trade minister was reprimanded, as were the officials for having complied with his instruction. But HMG stood behind the guarantee.

The Northern Ireland Protocol

A Northern Ireland Minister, Kevin Poots, ordered his officials to cease work on the construction of Border Control Posts required by the NI Protocol. They refused. Further detail is in chapter 2.2.8.1.

Rendition

I understand that Jack Straw's and other Ministers' decisions that the UK would cooperate with requests in 2004 to transfer terrorist suspects to American custody did not involve UK illegality.

An earlier example of rendition was the forced removal of individuals from a British Overseas Territory, the Chagos Islands, which host an American base on Diego Garcia. Again, as no UK laws were broken, I suspect that British civil servants were permitted to accept Ministers' decisions.

The Johnson Government

We may in due course add Boris Johnson's Prime Ministership to the above list. Well informed observers and commentators suggested that the 2019-22 government may have been the least serious, least effective and most dishonest administration in British history. Most of Johnson's lies aimed to avoid taking personal responsibility for policy failures, or to defend indefensible behaviour such as partying during the Covid pandemic.

Even more serious, perhaps, were Mr Johnson's attempts to prorogue (suspend) Parliament so as to avoid scrutiny at the height of the 2029 Brexit crisis, and two attempts to legislate to evade responsibility for unwelcome aspects of the post-Brexit legal agreement with the European Union that he himself had praised and signed.

At the time of writing, shortly after Mr Johnson's resignation in the summer of 2022, the extent to which he had involved (corrupted?) the civil service remained unclear, though the Sue Gray 'Partygate' report[52] showed that many senior officials had partied alongside the Prime Minister when most of the population were scrupulously following Covid lockdown

---

[52] https://www.civilservant.org.uk/library/2022-Sue_Gray-Partygate_report.pdf

guidelines. Here is David Allen Green's 2022 description of Boris Johnson's government before Mr Johnson resigned:

> The real problem with this government is not that it acts unlawfully or illegally. The problem is that it acts as if it is an outlaw - that for the government, law does not apply in the first place.
>
> It is not so much that the government cares about breaking any law, or about whether it has any legal basis for what it does. Instead, the government does not see law as even applying to it. To use a lovely Scottish word - the government acts as if it is *'outwith'* the law.
>
> The law applies to little people, and not this government. *'Law and Order'* is a campaigning slogan, but not a principle of government.
>
> This government engages in three types of lawlessness.
>
> - First, it often conducts itself without any lawful basis.
>
> - Second, it seeks to introduce legislation that will enable it to freely break the law.
>
> - Third, it permits law-breaking at the highest level.
>
> It is difficult to imagine a government with less respect for law, and for the rule of law.
>
> This is not so much a government of law breakers, but a government of outlaws.
>
> The law is an inconvenience which can be disregarded as and when it is inconvenient.

International Law

Northern Ireland Secretary Brandon Lewis conceded in 2020 that draft post-Brexit legislation (the Internal Market Bill) would, if enacted, breach the Brexit Withdrawal Agreement in a "specific and limited way". This led the Permanent

Secretary to the Government Legal Department, Sir Jonathan Jones, to resign. The most concerning elements of the Bill were later removed.

Three years later, ministers introduced draft legislation (concerning the removal of asylum seeks to Rwanda) which also appeared to breach international laws and treaties. As of January 2024, this legislation is still going through Parliament.

The implications for civil servants are considered at Chapter 2.2.8.1 above.

4.5 What should you do if you believe that a previously legitimate government is edging towards authoritarianism?

Brian Klaas observed that many of the leaders we loathe most were elected by our fellow citizens - from Hitler and Papa Doc Duvalier to Hugo Chavez, Rodrigo Duterte and Vladimir Putin.

> 'Corruptible people are disproportionately drawn to power, disproportionately good at wriggling their way into it and disproportionately likely to cling onto it once they've got it[53].'

What should civil servants do if an authoritarian gains power in the UK? Here is the classic answer, again from that 1983 Reith Lecture:

> Notwithstanding the loyalty of a civil servant to the government, his conscience should clearly require him to oppose actions which are either unlawful, unconstitutional, or which involve some great affront to human values. In the last analysis he must be prepared to resign his

---

[53] Leaders, and how to get the right ones. Sunday Times 16 January 2022.

appointment. But in such circumstances, I believe, he should be relieved of his normal obligation to refrain from commenting on policies for which he may have drafted official advice.

Stefan Czerniawski offered a fascinating analytical framework in Civil Servants Civilly Serve[54] in which starts by considering the boundaries to the legitimacy of politicians' decisions. He then considers how civil servants might respond if and when previously legitimate governments develop clear authoritarian tendencies.

Here are some extracts, with emphasis added:

- 'There is a simple answer, which is to carry on regardless. That is the answer still being assumed, based fundamentally on the idea that the government remains the government until it stops being the government and that, for as long as it does so, it is not for the civil service to look behind the formalities of its continuing existence or to question its authority.

- That position has some attractions: we don't want to be in a world where the civil service takes it on itself to decide whether it likes a government enough to be prepared to work for it. But there is also a profound weakness … **There is no shortage of examples, historical and modern, of states which have kept the forms of democratic government while edging towards authoritarianism. The difficulty is that when those forms fall away, it's generally too late to do much about it**. Before that point, though, there is inevitably judgement and ambiguity, with a very understandable temptation to see the continuity of what is legitimate and fail to see the discontinuity to what is illegitimate.

- What should civil servants do if those boundaries are reached and crossed? In principle the answer to that is simple. **At the point**

[54] https://www.publicstrategist.com/2019/10/civil-servants-civilly-serve/

any civil servant judges that the democratic legitimacy of Ministers has broken down, they must also accept that their ethical authority has also broken down. Whatever a civil servant does after that, they do as an independent moral agent, personally responsible for their decisions and actions. They may nevertheless choose to continue, accepting that responsibility. Or they may choose to walk away.

- The institution, of course will remain. Authoritarian governments have civil services, just as democratic ones do. But the surface form hides a profound difference. In such a civil service, loyalty is ultimately to the holders of power, not to the idea of good government, and the consequences are very different. Those who choose to be part of them are choosing to accept those consequences.

Alexandra Hall Hall agrees:-

- There will always be ambiguity — because who is to determine what is unlawful, unconscionable, or unethical? There will always be a different point of view. In many cases, the government may not actually be breaking the law, but nevertheless is acting in a manner which wilfully deceives the public over the true nature and consequences of its policies. Arguably, civil servants, in such cases, have a duty to speak out to ensure the electorate has the facts, but this runs the risk of civil servants being perceived as being political, or as trying to influence an election.

- In such circumstances, where doubt will always exist and criticism is almost certain, the only viable solution for a conflicted civil servant is to be accountable to themselves. Ultimately, the decision has to come down to a matter of personal judgment and conscience. As I put it in my own resignation letter, "each person has to find their own level of comfort." You don't have the right to change policy — that is for elected politicians and the ultimate verdict of voters. But you do have a right to your own personal conscience, and a right not to be a part of something you believe to be unethical.

Examples are thankfully rare, at least in the US and UK. But many from across the political spectrum have recently been able to point to some very worrying signs of authoritarianism in both the Trump administration and in the Johnson Government's lack of interest in rational decision making[55] and disdain for the courts and for Parliament[56]. Two important Lords committees have published reports respectively entitled

- Government by Diktat: A call to return power to Parliament[57] - and

- Democracy Denied? The urgent need to rebalance power between Parliament and the Executive[58].

I would therefore class Jonathan Jones' resignation as a response to excessive authoritarianism. Mr Jones was the chief civil service lawyer who resigned in September 2020 over the government's announcement that it intended to breach international law "in a limited and specific way". Interviewed later he said that his view, aside from the legal principle involved, was that the approach was ...

"completely bonkers and hugely damaging ...

... the government... was utterly disreputable [in] saying publicly that it was prepared ... to break the terms of the treaty which it had

---

[55] Hannah Arendt believes that authoritarian leaders are incapable of the serious thinking and analysis that is involved rational decision making.
[56] Historian Richard J Evans wrote that 'democracies die when politicians give up on their own parliaments' and that 'By proroguing [Parliament], Johnson signals his contempt for MPs'.
[57] https://committees.parliament.uk/publications/7941/documents/82225/default/
[58] https://committees.parliament.uk/publications/7960/documents/82286/default/

concluded and indeed, implemented into UK law only months before. That seemed to me to be disgraceful".

He said in a subsequent interview that he was perfectly satisfied that he did the right thing but stressed that:

> "I never, for a moment, tried to persuade anybody else that they should go. Plenty of people provided moral and personal support but in the end, this was a highly personal decision for me, and others took their own decisions. Because the business of government has to go on."

4.6 The Effectiveness Trap

Can an unhappy official achieve more by leaving (perhaps with significant publicity) - or by staying and seeking to improve things from within?

Not everyone who feels conflicted over government policy chooses to leave. Some make the decision to stay, and try to be a force for good from within. Alexandra Hall Hall quotes ex-US Ambassador Volker who does not think it is appropriate for civil servants to resign simply as a way of protest: He reserved his strongest criticism for those whom he believes tried to undermine the Trump administration from within, because in his view that only exacerbated distrust and fed the narrative of the existence of a deep state:

> "The only reason to resign is as a matter of personal choice. It's not about changing the world but whether in good conscience you can continue what you are doing. The U.S. and U.K. are democracies, and the people who are elected have the right to decide. They have the right to make policy. If you don't like it, that's your issue. You can express yourself and have a clear conscience, but you can't expect it to change policy."

Mark Esper was US Secretary of Defense reporting to Donald Trump. Here are a few paragraphs from his autobiography *A Sacred Oath*:

At times like this, I asked myself why I didn't resign. This was the existential question of the Trump administration: Why did good people stay even after the president suggested or pressed us to do things that were reckless, or foolish, or just plain wrong? Why did we remain even after he made outrageous or false statements, or denigrated our people, our departments, or us?

I wrestled with these questions many times during my tenure, and especially in the months following the events of June 1. It demanded a lot of soul-searching, reaching back in my upbringing, my education at West Point, and my training in the Army, studying historical examples, speaking with my predecessors in both parties, thinking hard about my oath, and talking it through with my wife. One more than one occasion, Leah would say to me, "As your wife, please quit. As an American citizen, please stay."

Quitting in outrage would have made me feel good in the moment – it would have saved me a ton of stress and criticism. News outlets and social media would likely hail me as a "resistance" hero. However, I didn't think it was the right thing to do *for our country*. And as I told a reporter once near the end of my tenure, "my soldiers don't get to quit" when the going gets tough, so I won't either. I agonized nonetheless. Many of us did.

There was another major concern I had to factor into the equation: Who would replace me? There likely wasn't enough time for the President to nominate and the Senate to confirm a new defense secretary. Nevertheless, Trump could certainly place a true loyalist as acting secretary. And given enough time, real damage could be done. We saw this earlier in the year when he installed Ric Grenell as the acting Director of National Intelligence. There were a number of people in the administration who would willingly do Trump's bidding, and probably even his more extreme dictates, and it deeply concerned me.

James Thomson famously described 'the effectiveness trap' in his analysis of the disastrous Vietnam War – *How Could Vietnam Happen? – An Autopsy* – and it makes for both entertaining and sobering reading: The effectiveness trap is …

> … the trap that keeps men from speaking out, as clearly or often as they might, within the government. And it is the trap that keeps men from resigning in protest and airing their dissent outside the government. The most important asset that a man brings to bureaucratic life is his 'effectiveness', a mysterious combination of training, style, and connections. The most ominous complaint that can be whispered of a bureaucrat is: "I'm afraid Charlie's beginning to lose his effectiveness". To preserve your effectiveness, you must decide where and when to fight the mainstream of policy; … . The inclination to remain silent or to acquiesce in the presence of the great men – to live to fight another day, to give on this issue so that you can be "effective" on later issues – is overwhelming.

Former FBI Director James Comey also summarised the problem very well:-

> It starts with your sitting silent while [President Trump] lies, both in public and private, making you complicit by your silence. In meetings with him, his assertions about what "everyone thinks" and what is "obviously true" wash over you, unchallenged … because he's the president and he rarely stops talking. As a result, Mr. Trump pulls all of those present into a silent circle of assent. …
>
> I must have agreed that he had the largest inauguration crowd in history because I didn't challenge that. Everyone must agree that he has been treated very unfairly. The web building never stops. From the private circle of assent, it moves to public displays of personal fealty at places

like cabinet meetings. While the entire world is watching, you do what everyone else around the table does — you talk about how amazing the leader is and what an honor it is to be associated with him.

So you are well and truly trapped. A pathetic courtier if you stay. A hypocrite if you eventually leave.

Mr Comey presumably has some sympathy for Dr Deborah Bix who was forced to sit, looking down at her shoes, whilst President Trump suggested that Americans might inject bleach in order to treat COVID-19. Others, however, were not so forgiving and argued that she could have saved hundreds of thousands of lives if she had stood up to the President during the pandemic's first surge.

In short, it behoves us all to bear in mind the reflections of the protagonist in Ivan Klima's *Judge on Trial*:- "We commit crimes, or at least we acquiesce in them, so we can go on leading normal lives. But we can never live normally again once we are implicated."

Chapter 5
Blunders and Criticism

Previous chapters have described the role of the civil servants within the UK constitution and have focussed in particular in the relationship between officials, Ministers and Parliament. But no-one can sensibly claim that this *Westminster Model* of government has produced uniformly good results. This chapter explores what has gone wrong.

In no particular order, I have divided the analysis in this chapter into a number of separate (if slightly overlapping) parts.

5.1. What happened to Speaking Truth to Power?
5.2. Government Blunders

5.1 What happened to Speaking Truth to Power?

A fundamental feature of the Westminster Model of Government is that Ministers are not free to ignore official expertise. "Ministers have a duty to give fair consideration and due weight to informed and impartial advice from civil servants, as well as to other considerations and advice in reaching policy decisions"[59]. Officials must accordingly not hesitate to 'speak truth to power'[60]. Ministers should, for instance, be told in no uncertain terms if officials believe that their programs could not be delivered within the resources and timescales allocated to them.

But many critics argue that the modern delivery-focussed civil service has become much less good at challenging Ministers, and might even have become somewhat politicised. The initial Universal Credit program, for example, seemed unrealistic. Departments' press releases are becoming a little too economical with the truth. And Permanent Secretaries are agreeing too easily to implement Ministers' short-sighted management decisions.

---

[59] This is from the Ministerial Code - https://www.civilservant.org.uk/library/2019-MINIS-TERIAL-CODE-FINAL.pdf

[60] https://www.civilservant.org.uk/richborne_publishing.html#STtP

In total contrast, however, other powerful critics - including many Ministers - think that the civil service is far too obstructive. They would be pleased if - but do not believe that - the civil service has indeed become more willing to energetically carry out Ministers' wishes. It is not many years since *The Times* reported *"Whitehall in Worst Crisis … '[officials] think it's their job just to say "No" … "The Civil Service sees itself as a check and balance within the political system, and that's a problem."* Many other governments have felt similar frustration. This hardly suggests that officials have forgotten their challenge function.

One difficulty is that we just don't know whether the challenge function of the civil service has indeed been degraded over time, and if so whether that is a good thing. It has long been thought that one necessary consequence of the close and occasional stressful relationship between officials and Ministers has been the invisibility of civil service advice. But how can we resolve the conflicting arguments, and reduce the amount of blundering, without piercing Whitehall's veil? The rest of this chapter, and the next one, explore these questions in some detail.

5.2 Government Blunders

No Government can claim to be 'blunder-free'. The British Government can certainly be criticised for the way in which it helped carve up the Middle East after the First World War and carved up India after the Second World War. The American Government's reaction to 9/11 was arguably inappropriate. All three of these policy decisions have dreadful consequences decades later.

And yet each of those three blunders can be explained by the politics of the time, where domestic pressures made it very difficult, verging on impossible, for decisions to be taken after careful analysis. The same cannot be said of the extensive list of British policy and delivery failures over recent years. A number of these were identified in Richard Bacon and Christopher Hope's *Conundrum* and Anthony King's and Ivor Crewe's *The Blunders of our Governments*, both published in 2013.

The King/Crewe book analyses the causes of a wide range of pre-2013 blunders, including:

- the poll tax,

- personal pensions mis-selling,

- the Child Support Agency,

- the UK's exit from the Exchange Rate Mechanism,

- The Millennium Dome,

- Individual Learning Accounts,

- Tax Credits,

- the Assets Recovery Agency,

- the farmers' Single Payment Scheme,

- various IT projects[61],

- the London Underground public-private partnership, and

- identity cards.

---

[61] Successive administrations had wasted "obscene" amounts of money on government information technology, according to the Commons Public Accounts Committee reporting in July 2011. "Over-reliance on a few large contractors and poor public sector purchasing and management skills have produced a recipe for rip-offs".

I have prepared my own list of other blunders. The full list can be found on my civil servant website[62] and a shorter list is below.

- Ministers decided to build two new aircraft carriers, despite the money not being available to pay for them. The incoming coalition government subsequently decided to proceed with the construction of the ships but not to equip them with aircraft for some years.

- It was difficult to understand the real reasons for the apparent failure of successive governments properly to equip our armed forces in Afghanistan. Was this another example of a failure to resolve the underlying tension between Ministers' wish to provide all possible support for our troops and Ministers' equally strong desire to save money?

- The performance of a small part of the civil service came under severe scrutiny when Virgin Group forced the Department for Transport (DfT) to withdraw its offer of the West Coast franchise to First Group, blaming civil servants for failures in economic and financial modelling and - it was hinted - for concealing the problems and/or giving too strong assurances to Ministers that all was well.

- The UK's bid for the Olympics assumed a public sector funding package of £2.4 billion. London 2012 eventually cost the public purse around £6 billion more than the original estimate.

- In September 2013, the NAO published a devastating report on DWP's 'over-ambitious' Universal Credit program managed by a team with a' fortress mentality' in which 'only good news was allowed'

And then, whatever you think of the post-2010 'austerity', the UK's decision to leave the European Union, or the politics of the Johnson government:

---

[62] https://www.civilservant.org.uk/library/all_blunders.pdf

- the NHS, social care, transport infrastructure and may other central and local government services are currently in a very bad state,

- there are few who believe that Brexit implementation has gone smoothly, and

- the government's preparation for, and initial response to, the Covid pandemic was seriously flawed[63].

Many politicians and others thought that one solution to Westminster's obvious weakness might be to delegate much decision-making to arm's length experts in the form of regulators. The experience of post-privatisation regulation of telecoms, energy etc. convinced them it was much better to have such decisions taken by apolitical experts who were willing to think long term and well beyond the electoral cycle. This thinking lay behind Chancellor Gordon Brown's decision to delegate interest rate-setting to the Bank of England. Crucially, too, it meant that Ministers could avoid blame when energy prices rose, or patients were refused access to expensive medicines, or mortgages became more expensive.

These trends are discussed in greater depth in my *Understanding Regulation website*[64]. But regulators, too, turned out to be flawed - or under-resourced - or under-powered - and this inevitably led to led to

- the 2008 financial crisis,

- the Jimmy Saville and Rotherham child abuse scandals,

- the Mid-Staffs Hospital scandal,

- the Grenfell Tower disaster, and

- many more failures of regulatory systems which central

---

[63] https://www.civilservant.org.uk/skills-crises.html
[64] https://www.regulation.org.uk/index.html

Government had designed and for which central Government retained final responsibility.

5.3 So .. What Caused These Blunders?

King and Crewe, in particular, seemed genuinely puzzled by the fact that our politicians and civil servants are so prone to serious blundering:

> [British governments] screw up more often than most people seem to realise. .. Governments of all parties appear equally blunder-prone. .. in spite of government's incessant blundering, the United Kingdom is in many ways a well-governed country. [The majority of] our political leaders … are genuinely concerned with both the British people's welfare and the country's long term future. .. Compared with the political elites of some countries .. most British politicians and civil servants are models of both rectitude and public-spiritedness. .. these very qualities make the frequency with which they commit blunders the more surprising and disappointing."

They went on to divide the causes into two main groups – human errors and system failures – but they do not specifically criticise civil servants. According to its index, 'civil servants' and 'officials' are mentioned on only five pages of a 400+ page book. This seems odd. After all, the Senior Civil Service outnumbers Ministers by around 40 to 1 and so can hardly avoid taking a share of the responsibility for the blundering. And isn't it supposed to be brilliant at analysing problems and 'speaking truth to power' - and being heard?

Richard Bacon and Christopher Hope (in *Conundrum*) spend much more time looking at the civil service, and being unimpressed:

'One of the most enduring paradoxes is how the civil service manages to take some of the most intellectually gifted people in the whole country and repeatedly make such a hash of things ... it is rather strange that such people seem able to put up with the sustained mediocrity and industrial scale cock-ups that we have witnessed. ... Here would seem to be a classic case of the government squandering one of its most valuable resources - its people.'

One King & Crewe theme was government's failure to learn from previous failures - or even reconsider policies when they are going badly wrong. Neither Ministers nor officials are incentivised to identify and resolve problems as policies are being rolled out, because they will then be associated with what will be characterised as a mistake or a failure. Similarly, they will later not acknowledge that a failure has happened, for fear of suffering political or career damage. This clearly inhibits learning.

There were also systemic problems with the delivery of the government's various programs. Professor King, writing in the Financial Times in April 2012, commented that:-

'Part of the problem is the sheer velocity with which most Ministers evidently feel compelled to act. With the prime minister either urging them on – or, more probably, not restraining them – they advance rapidly and simultaneously on all fronts: NHS reform, local government reform, law reform, school reform, planning reform, welfare reform, the list goes on. The spectacle resembles a 19th-century cavalry charge, with some horsemen and their mounts inevitably cut down.

The contrast between Mr Cameron and Margaret Thatcher could hardly be more striking. He is hell bent for leather and makes a speech almost every day as though to ram home the point. Mrs Thatcher was at least as radical a prime minister but far more focused and cautious.

She had a clear sense of direction but travelled only slowly during the most successful phases of her premiership. Following her first electoral triumph in 1979, she was in office for fully three years before launching her most ambitious projects: trade union reform and privatisation. It was not until 1982 that she abandoned her step-by-step approach towards reforming the unions and encouraged Norman Tebbit (who needed little encouragement) to radically overhaul trade-union law. It was not until 1984, well into her second term, that her government began to undertake the wholesale privatisation of state-owned industries, starting with British Telecom. She looked before she leapt, until, to her cost, she lost the habit.'

5.4 The World is Now Very Different

The previous section makes the case that the Westminster/ Haldane system has failed to provide good government over many decades. But the world around, and indeed government itself, has changed out of all recognition since 1919. Is the *Westminster Model* still fit for purpose? Here is what some senior officials and others have said to me:-

In wider society:-

- Public and media have become much less deferential over several generations. This a good thing - but Ministers have responded by requiring Whitehall to become much more defensive, less open to considered criticism, and less willing to consider options before reaching policy conclusions.

- Freedom of Information has accordingly become seen as a threat instead of a codification of what should be done naturally.

- The media – including social media – are now so massive that government has to put a lot more effort into communications activity

– but, even so, we all know that a lie can travel half way around the world while the truth is still getting its boots on. Government pronouncements are therefore often rushed, and lack subtlety and accuracy.

- Globalisation, immigration and our past membership of the EU also mean that the government's audience is much more varied than in the past. This exposure to other cultures has many advantages but poses problems for the government's communications teams.

- There is some evidence that society is becoming more polarised, which can lead to ignorance & cognitive dissonance on both sides of the arguments.

- Prosperity has generated a number of 'wicked policy issues' as we have more to spend on food, drugs and alcohol – and on mobile phones and other consumer goods that are so tempting for the criminally minded.

Within Whitehall:-

- Ministers don't understand implications of the cuts in staff numbers that they have ordered. The resultant loss of experience will mean that they will not have civil service support when they need it, nor of the experience/quality that they need.

- Senior officials in particular are now over-stretched, and have little time for getting out and understanding the policy areas and sectors within which they work.

- Civil servants have learned that there is little point in challenging major decisions, however, short-sighted. They instead focus on controlling the (devil in) the detail.

- The market-based approach to appointments led to greater turbulence and less depth of knowledge.

- HMG in many areas no longer acts as a supplier; it instead buys services from and for others. But its procurement and negotiations skills are still pretty weak, and its lawyers are too often out-gunned by their expensive heavyweight private sector opponents.

- 'Fast stream' recruits no longer have a career anchor/home department – they are all nominally employed by HMRC - and their 6 month appointments, rotating around departments, mean they can't gain a deep understanding of any one department's issues, nor gain experience in a Minister's Private Office.

Many of the above comments are echoed by academic commentators:-

Professor Jeremy Richardson makes these points:

- There have been important changes within government departments, namely a change in the balance of power between senior civil servants on the one hand, and Ministers and their Special Advisers on the other.

- Many Ministers (and their external advisers, both official and informal) arrive in office with a thorough knowledge of their policy portfolio and their own strong priorities on what policy change is needed. This has led to a shift from civil servants warning Ministers and keeping them out of trouble, reflecting the traditional risk aversion normally attributed to British government, towards 'carriers' of Ministerial ideas, willing to try to implement policies even when lacking broad policy community support.

- There are big risks inherent in the new policy style under which consultation is much more constrained.

- Professor Richardson quotes David Halpern (Head of Number 10's Behavioural Insights Team) as describing life behind the shiny black door of Number 10 as akin to a hospital Accident & Emergency Department:- 'in such a world, there's often not the time,

nor the patience, for the answer to be "more research needed"'
There is more than a hint here of a 'pop-up' style of policymak-
ing where chaps (mostly!) with seemingly clever policy ideas get to
implement them without the need to consider the views of, or seek
the support of, the affected interests.

And here are some more extracts from Professor Anthony
King's *Who Governs Britain?*

- Ministers now] believe … that if they are to impress … they must
  constantly be seen to be taking initiatives [and] if change is desirable … then it is desirable *now* not at some unspecified time in the
  future … Post-Thatcher Ministers are characterised by their impa-
  tience. [They] have no incentive at all to think about the longer
  term future.

- The traditional British civil service … was dynamic. Generations
  of senior civil servants regarded it as part of their mission … to
  promote causes.

- [The post-Thatcher] change of role meant a corresponding
  change in the role and mind-set of officials. From now on, officials
  were to be civil *servants* in reality, at their master's beck and call, ea-
  ger to do their master's bidding. … By the time New Labour came
  to power in 1997, there were few if any of the old style mandarins
  still in place.

- Many Ministers, with much expected of them and suspicious of
  their officials, turned for help and advice to … special advisers …
  and … think tanks.

- More than two decades after the fall of Margaret Thatcher, the
  vast majority of officials, including the most senior, give the impression of having settled into their new, more subordinate role.
  … … "We wanted", one of them said, "to avoid a Sir Humphrey
  image. We became afraid to say "No, Minister". [Another said …]
  "Can-do man was in and wait-a-minute man was out.

- ... officials, once the embodiments of departmental continuity, are now at least as transient as their political masters and therefore at least as liable not to have a very firm grasp of what they are doing.

- [A Cabinet Minister complained] that his own department's collective memory was so short ... that "... people deal only with the instant they are living in, rather than drawing on any kind of history or knowledge of the detail and background to a particular issue."

Professor Kakabadse says that:

- [Senior] civil servants admit to misunderstandings, misjudgements, feeling inhibited to speak up and, in certain circumstances and with particular Secretaries of State, not knowing how to speak truth to power.

- Even middle-ranking and more junior civil servants described feeling defensive and reluctant to offer opinion, fearing reprimand or being viewed in a negative light.

Longer excerpts from these three academics' writing may be found on my website[65].

5.5 Whitehall Thinks it Knows Best

There is another possible problem, seldom recognised by those in the Westminster Bubble.

Many critics, including a fair number of modern politicians, argue that political elites have for too long been making decisions without reference to the public. The role of the electorate has been to do little more than legitimise politics, rather than to be involved in politics.

---

[65] https://www.civilservant.org.uk/library/The_Westminster_Model-Academic_Commentary.pdf

The Westminster Model of government, they say, is to a great extent predicated on the view that 'Government knows best'. It assumes that the public does not have the information necessary to make the right decisions. Key decisions are therefore taken by Ministers and/or officials, approved as necessary by Parliament.

Secrecy is supposed to ensure that the right decisions are made in the interests of the people. A responsible government is empowered to take strong decisive action, even when opposed by a majority of the population. This is a leadership rather than participatory view of democracy, but it is legitimised by regular democratic elections, when representatives can be held to account for their decisions.

The Haldane Model (mutually interdependent Ministers and officials) also encourages concentration of power at heart of the British political system and 'Government by the elite'. This concentration of power means that senior civil servants can be powerful whilst simultaneously maintaining the polite fiction they are "only advisers". Politicians can, at the same time, continue to maintain that they are really taking all the decisions. In practice, of course, the relative power and influence of senior officials varies very much from Government to Government, and with the characters and experience of the officials and their Ministers. But critics argue that the Westminster/Haldane model is in effect a facade which works to the benefit of both politicians and civil servants, but which disguises the truth from the population at large.

Shielding the inner workings of government can also easily morph into hypocrisy and cover up. The Establishment used to be pretty good at hiding its infidelities, homosexual activity and drunken misbehaviour. A good thing, many would say. But it may also have been pretty good at hiding police corruption, paedophilia and other nasties. Not quite the same?

And what about the Establishment's ability to resist policies that it regards as dangerous or illiberal, such as leaving the EU, ditching Trident, bringing back hanging or cutting immigration and overseas aid? Whitehall, like so many other large organisations, already harbours a good deal of groupthink - often described as 'showing good judgment'. No promotion-hungry Whitehall civil servant was ever going to admit to voting for UKIP, or agreeing with the Scottish Nationalists. A good thing, some would say. Is there not something to be said for initial civil service resistance to the more dramatic or far-reaching pressures for change, at least so as to give the electorate and Ministers time to think again? But it is hardly democracy in action.

There were critics of the secretive nature of the British civil service as long ago as the 19th Century. Sir James Stephen doubted that any bright individual would wish to pursue a career in which ...

> 'He must devote all his talents ... to measures, some of which he will assuredly disapprove, without having the slightest power to prevent them; and to some of which he will most essentially contribute, without having any share whatsoever in the credit bestowed on others, ... and if any accident should make him notorious enough to become the suspected

author of any unpopular act, he must silently submit to the reproach, even though it is totally unmerited by him'.

The modern electorate certainly seem to believe that 'the Westminster Village' is incompetent and/or out of touch with the concerns of those who live outside cosmopolitan London. They see a hypocritical establishment, much more inclined to tell voters to 'do what I say' rather than 'do what I do'. This seems to be leading to declining numbers voting in elections, and declining membership of the main political parties. Many voters seem to be totally disengaged from politics. There was (and is) little persistent anger with those responsible for the financial crisis, for the Iraq war and for the approaching 200,000 Covid deaths, let alone for the other blunders listed above. The *Institute for Government* has reported that there is no correlation between things that the public thinks that government 'should' prioritise and what it 'does' prioritise.

It seems, therefore, that Whitehall needs to work much harder to involve citizens in decision-making. This implies opening to public scrutiny the debates between Ministers and officials.

5.6 Whitehall Does Know Best! - The Case for the Defence

Despite the above blunders, there are many who continue to believe in the fundamental strength of the Westminster/Haldane model. Commentators such as Daniel Finkelstein and Matthew Parris argue that the public do not understand the complexity and long-term nature of government. Politicians (they say) know when they are blundering. They know what needs to be done – at least in the 'wicked areas' such as the environment, tax, foreign policy, pensions, drugs. But they just don't know how to get re-elected after doing it.

Politicians (they say) are not unaware of evidence, but they are often forced to ignore it given the pressure to be re-elected and the influence of pressure and focus groups, and social and other media. Greater civil service accountability, for instance, would not help. The faults in the system (in their view) lie outside government in the ill-informed or unforgiving nature of the electorate and media. Politicians and officials should be allowed to debate, quite privately, how to negotiate the tricky shoals of public opinion.

5.7 Would it Help if Civil Servants were Publicly Accountable?

It is not only politicians who live in the Westminster Village. Is it not time that officials became more accountable for their advice and their actions – or absence of action? Some of them have been intimately involved in the ineffective planning, in ignoring warnings, and in delivering the faulty policies. Surely they cannot avoid taking some of the blame?

It is interesting to consider how officials would react to greater public scrutiny. Many of them, I suspect, would have no problem in principle. Those who have been Agency Chief Executives, or have led Non-Ministerial Government

Departments, have generally enjoyed the experience, and have been glad to account for their decisions and performance both in Parliament and via the media.

And Accounting Officers and others are often very uncomfortable (though they seldom show it) when faced with the real world consequences of Ministerial decisions. One example was the Public Accounts Committee tearing into Ministry of Justice officials for failing to identify all the unintended consequences and costs arising out of Ministers' decision to lop £300m off the legal aid budget – and to do it very quickly. I'll bet a pound to a penny that officials would much rather have dragged their feet and not implemented this policy at this speed, and I'll bet they were acutely aware of its consequences, not least for the disadvantaged. Would we not be better governed if the public had had access to those officials' advice and concerns, which might have helped ensure that Ministers did not achieve their policy objectives?

Some MPs are not too worried about exposing differences between officials and Ministers. Cabinet Office Minister Francis Maude saw no problem in such public debates. "A Minister who is confident about what he or she has decided should have no problem in publicly defending it". By way of example, he said that he would like to see much more use made of the 'constitutional safety valve' of written Ministerial Directions to Accounting Officers. They should become 'much more normal' and no longer seen as the nuclear, relationship-destroying option. Indeed, he believed that the fear of using Directions may well have led to officials failing to challenge decisions with which they are uncomfortable, but then failing to implement those decisions.

Lord Maude's and others' encouragement does seem to be having some effect. A number of interesting recent developments are discussed in chapter 6.

5.8 It's Just as Bad (or Worse) Elsewhere

Before we get too depressed about the state of British government, it is important to be aware that there are plenty of other blundering governments, so maybe the 'Westminster Model' is not solely, or even mainly, to blame for the UK's dismal performance. Here are some extracts from James Thomson's entertaining and sobering analysis of the disaster that was the Vietnam War: *How Could Vietnam Happen?: An Autopsy*[66] . In his article, Thomson identifies a number of factors that shaped Kennedy and Johnson's disastrous Vietnam policy - and many if not all of them can be seen to contribute to other major blunders in the UK and elsewhere.

The first factor was ignorance of prior history and false perceptions of current developments in the Far East, exacerbated by the absence (or banishment) of real Vietnam or Indochina expertise.

> "Here the underlying cause was the "closed politics" of policy-making as issues become hot: the more sensitive the issue, and the higher it rises in the bureaucracy, the more completely the experts are excluded while the harassed senior generalists take over (that is, the Secretaries,

---

[66] https://www.civilservant.org.uk/library/1968-James_Thomson-How_Could_Vietnam_Happen.pdf

Undersecretaries, and Presidential Assistants). The frantic skimming of briefing papers in the back seats of limousines is no substitute for the presence of specialists; furthermore, in times of crisis such papers are deemed "too sensitive" even for review by the specialists.

Another underlying cause of this banishment, as Vietnam became more critical, was the replacement of the experts, who were generally and increasingly pessimistic, by men described as "can-do guys," loyal and energetic fixers unsoured by expertise."

Then there was the Effectiveness Trap (see chapter 4.6) and Bureaucratic Inertia, ...

"... the collective inertia produced by the bureaucrat's view of his job. At State, the average "desk officer" inherits from his predecessor our policy toward Country X; he regards it as his function to keep that policy intact —under glass, untampered with, and dusted—so that he may pass it on in two to four years to his successor. And such curatorial service generally merits promotion within the system. (Maintain the status quo, and you will stay out of trouble.) In some circumstances, the inertia bred by such an outlook can act as a brake against rash innovation. But on many issues, this inertia sustains the momentum of bad policy and unwise commitments—momentum that might otherwise have been resisted within the ranks."

... not to mention Wishful Thinking and Bureaucratic Detachment

"By this I mean what at best might be termed the professional callousness of the surgeon (and indeed, medical lingo—the "surgical strike" for instance—seemed to crop up in the euphemisms of the times). In Washington the semantics of the military muted the reality of war for the civilian policy-makers. In quiet, air-conditioned, thick-carpeted rooms, such terms as "systematic pressure," "armed reconnaissance," "targets of opportunity," and even "body count" seemed to breed a sort of games-theory detachment. ...

Perhaps the biggest shock of my return to Cambridge, Massachusetts, was the realization that the young men, the flesh and blood I taught and saw on these university streets, were potentially some of the numbers on the charts of those faraway planners. In a curious sense, Cambridge is closer to this war than Washington."

Last, but not least there was the investment in Human Ego.

"Men who have participated in a decision develop a stake in that decision. As they participate in further, related decisions, their stake increases. It might have been possible to dissuade a man of strong self-confidence at an early stage of the ladder of decision; but it is infinitely harder at later stages since a change of mind there usually involves implicit or explicit repudiation of a chain of previous decisions.

To put it bluntly: at the heart of the Vietnam calamity is a group of able, dedicated men who have been regularly and repeatedly wrong— and whose standing with their contemporaries, and more important, with history, depends, as they see it, on being proven right. These are not men who can be asked to extricate themselves from error.

5.9 Some Structural Issues

Finally … it is important to recognise that the issues discussed in this book are part of a wider discussion involving many constitutional and political issues.

Numerous attempts to achieve significant 'civil service reform' have failed because they have been too narrowly focussed. They have in particular not been willing to consider changing the relationship between civil servants and Ministers, and between both of these and Parliament. This problem is discussed in more detail on my *Civil Servant website*[67].

---

[67] https://www.civilservant.org.uk/csr-homepage.html

There are also separate interesting questions concerning the effectiveness of Cabinet government. Does modern government need a strong centre and, if so, what does this do to the role of Cabinet Ministers - and of No.10? The 1960s Labour Government had two-day Cabinet meeting. Would that be unimaginable today, or a welcome development? A 2005 House of Commons Research Paper[68] discusses these issues in some detail.

Some argue, with compelling evidence, that there are fundamental problems with the nature of the British state. Nick Tyrone, for instance, commented in 2023[69] that:

'Britain is fundamentally poorly governed ... The current government wants to blame this on the civil service, but that's projection ... The vast majority of the dysfunction comes, sadly, from our elected officials ... This isn't a partisan point I'm making either. Labour governments tend to be just as bad as Tory ones.'

This argument was made at much greater and more devastating length by Ian Dunt in his book *How Westminster Works ... and Why It Doesn't.*

It is interesting, too, that recent developments have strengthened the position of senior officials who wish to challenge the feasibility of Ministers' policy decisions - that is the government's ability to carry out the proposed policy effectively and credibly. This is discussed further in chapter 6.

---

[68] https://www.civilservant.org.uk/library/2005-HoC-The_Centre_of_Government.pdf
[69] https://www.civilservant.org.uk/library/2023-Nick_Tyrone-This_week_in_Brexitland.pdf

Chapter 6
Increasing Accountability

Earlier chapters have suggested that UK Governments might 'blunder' less often if a light could be shone on their inner workings, and in particular on interactions between ministers and civil servants. Why should officials be sheltered from informed parliamentary and other external comment on their role in major failures? Should it not be possible for those harmed by such failures to tell whether:

- Ministers refused to listen to sensible advice, or

- Officials failed to communicate sensible advice in a persuasive way, or

- Officials advice was very poor?

The possibility of subsequent scrutiny might encourage senior officials to push back more strongly when they encounter obviously wrong-headed or excessively short-term Ministerial proposals.

This chapter accordingly summarises some tentative moves that have already taken place towards increased accountability for civil servants.

It also warns that progress will be slow unless and until Members of Parliament themselves improve the way they interact with both ministers and officials.

I have divided the discussion into these sections:

6.1. The Story So Far
6.2. Corporate Manslaughter
6.3. Policy Directions
6.4. Procedural Directions
6.5. Feasibility Directions
6.6. Senior Responsible Officers
6.7. Accounting Officer Assessments
6.8. Will We Notice the Difference?

6.1 The Story So Far

Whatever the strength of the arguments for and against greater civil service accountability, there does seem to be a long-term if almost imperceptible trend towards increasing the public accountability of the most senior officials.

The first sign of this trend was the creation of Next Steps Executive Agencies when the Thatcher administration decided that it was reasonable to hold officials rather than Ministers accountable for failures of administration. It was felt that the doctrine that Ministers should be held personally responsible for every failure in a department, however distant and minor, had never made much sense in theory or in practice. Ministers should certainly look for assurance that the right people and systems were in place, but they should not feel they need hands-on control. The more control they assert, the more they will attract blame for failures.

Next came a proliferation of regulators, charged with making many politically sensitive decisions independently of Ministers, including setting energy prices, encouraging competition in postal services, and deciding what medicines may be prescribed. The regulators are often criticised for being unelected, but their Boards and their staff are certainly much more accountable than their opposite numbers (and often ex-colleagues) in Whitehall departments.

Other developments which might have encouraged more effective accountability include:

- Corporate Manslaughter, Human Rights, and Freedom of Information legislation,

- the increased use of Judicial Review

- the Inquiries into events etc. such as Hillsborough, Bloody Sunday, Child Abuse and Grenfell Tower, often years after the events being investigated.

Parliamentary scrutiny has improved, too, since Departmental Select Committees were first established in 1979. Their Chairs are no longer appointed by the Government, and they have the opportunity (if they wish) to question senior officials about *Feasibility Directions* and *Accounting Officer Assessments*. These are two of five proposed or implemented innovations within government:-

- **Policy Directions** were intended to encourage Ministers to follow robust policy processes.

- **Procedural Directions** were intended to encourage Ministers (including the Prime Minister) to follow the processes outlined in the Cabinet Manual

- **Feasibility Directions** are intended to encourage Ministers to authorise expenditure only on feasible projects,

- **Senior Responsible Officer** appointments require senior officials in charge of major projects to report progress direct to Parliament (thus ensuring that officials would challenge projects with over-demanding objectives etc.)

- **Accounting Office Assessments** require senior officials to approve in advance all significant initiatives, policies, programmes and projects, and so be able to provide assurance to Parliament that those activities provide value for money and are feasible etc.

I look at each of these later on in this chapter, but I first return to the possible effect of the Corporate Manslaughter legislation.

6.2 Corporate Manslaughter etc.

Senior officials are increasingly aware of the threat of manslaughter and other criminal and civil litigation, but seem to be struggling to respond.

The problem is that civil servants will willingly implement policies which increase death rates (by increasing speed limits or cutting prison staffing numbers, for instance) but they would not follow an instruction that would lead to the death of a known individual. Can this distinction hold firm?

Here are some examples.

- Ministry of Defence civil servants discovered that they might be prosecuted for criminal negligence following the 2006 crash of an RAF Nimrod aircraft. The subsequent Inquiry held the MoD procurement team accountable for failure to maintain oversight of the cumulative and dangerous effect of changes to the aircraft. The report described an MoD stricken by "organisational trauma" induced by the overwhelming objective of finding savings. "There was no doubt that the culture of the time had switched. In the days of the RAF chief engineer in the 1990s, you had to be on top of airworthiness. By 2004 you had to be on top of your budget if you wanted to get ahead." Put shortly, the MoD had sacrificed safety to cut costs, and this had led to the deaths of 14 people. In the event, there were no prosecutions although compensation of £15m was paid. A book published in 2019 went further and claimed that a hundred British military personnel had died in avoidable accidents over the previous 35 years because of cost cutting etc. by the Ministry of Defence.

- The Times reported (8 February 2020) that the danger of a corporate manslaughter prosecution had been raised in 2011 when officials were discussing the removal of hard shoulders on some stretches of motorways. The consequential danger of a car being stranded in front of fast-running traffic caused a lawyer to ask "whether corporate manslaughter had been considered" if a motorist were to die as a result.

- The 2017 Grenfell Tower tragedy, in which 72 people died, is still being investigated, including by the police who might decide to bring prosecutions. Might this include the department responsible for drafting or enforcing building regulations?

- In April 2022 the High Court ruled unlawful the policy of discharging patients from hospitals to care homes during the Covid pandemic. Health Secretary Matt Hancock later admitted to the Covid Inquiry that the Government had not (as he had claimed in 2020) thrown their protective arms around care homes.

The above examples suggest that senior officials need to be aware of their departments' possible liability if asked to implement, or work within, policies which they believe likely to harm others. But it will be difficult to design sensible, practical advice and training.

Should civil servants also be concerned that they might individually be investigated following an avoidable death?

I am not aware that such an investigation has ever taken place but the General Medical Council has grappled with a similar problem. Its answer was not impressive:-

- Dr Bawa-Garba was a well-respected and experienced doctor who agreed in 2011 to work in an understaffed and unsafe hospital environment but then, under pressure, made mistakes which led to the death of a child. She was prosecuted and found guilty of manslaughter. The GMC in response issued guidelines telling doctors that if they were required to work in understaffed, unsafe environments then they must create a paper trail flagging that up. But this put doctors in the impossible position of being forced to choose between

- refusing to work in such circumstances, and therefore not only being in breach of contract but also potentially harming patients, or

- risking civil or even criminal action if they do choose to work, having identified the danger.

I am not aware that that advice was superseded, although Dr Bawa-Garba was eventually allowed to resume caring for patients.

6.3 Policy Directions

The Institute for Government was the first to suggest that it might be possible to improve civil service accountability by expanding the role of Ministerial Directions[70] beyond those which give ministerial cover for a decision to spend money which does not meet the tests of regularity, propriety, and value for money.

The Institute's 2011 report *Making Policy Better speaks for itself:*

> We propose adding a fourth Ministerial Direction:- poor policy process, where the Accounting Officer (usually the Permanent Secretary) is not satisfied that the fundamentals of policy making have been adequately observed. This recommendation builds on current practice. The Treasury currently recommends that AOs should exercise judgement on when they need to "take a principled decision".

> One of the standards they should use to make this judgement is whether "clear, well-reasoned timely and impartial advice" has been provided, and whether the decision is in line with the aims and objectives of their organisation – both of which relate closely to our proposed fundamentals. Furthermore, this new criterion could be seen as an extension of

---

[70] https://www.civilservant.org.uk/directions-overview.html

the current value for money criteria, since there is a good case that a poorly made policy will provide poor value for money.

The Treasury is already considering extending AOs' responsibilities to 'feasibility', but our proposal would also embrace the wider way in which policy is made.

Where the Minister wanted to override the objection, they could do so, but would need to give a 'policy direction'. Such a change would sharpen the incentives for both parties. AOs would act in the knowledge that they could be held to account by the departmental select committee for the quality of the policy process, whether or not a direction was issued.

Since the direction would be sent to the relevant select committee and published on the department's website, the Minister would be publicly accountable for taking action despite civil service concerns. The point of extending the AO remit in this way is not to ensure more directions are issued, but to make clear to officials, and in particular the head of department, that they must take responsibility for good process. **By extension, this will give Ministers a stronger incentive to observe good policy process**.

I have emphasised the final sentence above because it indirectly explains why there was very little chance that Ministers would accept this constraint on their ability to seek political advantage by making bold promises[71]. Indeed, I am not aware of any later consideration of the idea. However, as noted by the IfG, the Treasury were already examining the introduction of Feasibility Directions (see further below).

---

[71] Policy Directions might, for instance, have obstructed Prime Minister Cameron's Big Society and Prime Minister May's Social Mobility announcements. Peter Hennessy recalled that he had been told that the Big Society was more "a state of mind" than a specific idea. An official said that the Big Society announcement was "like publicising a new car badge without first designing the car"

6.4 Procedural Directions

In parallel with all the above, the Public Administration and Constitutional Affairs Committee supported a proposal from the *Better Government Initiative* informed by Chilcot's criticisms of Blair government decision-making before the Iraq War. The suggestion was that

- Prime Ministers should continue to be asked to consider, after appointment and after each election, how they propose to make important and sensitive policy decisions, including the way in which they expect to work with Cabinet colleagues, share legal advice, and the like. Their decisions should continue be recorded in an updated Cabinet Manual.

- However, unlike now, Ministers would know that they would be held to account if they were to deviate from the processes laid out in the Manual.

- This accountability would be ensured by having the Cabinet Secretary and/or individual Permanent Secretaries seek a 'Procedural Direction' when asked to support Ministers operating outside the terms of the Cabinet Manual.

- Unlike the already well-established Financial Directions, Procedural Directions might be kept quiet until the need for secrecy had passed, but the responsible Ministers would know that they would one day be held to account for their decision.

One example, had this mechanism already existed, might have been Tony Blair's failure to circulate pre-Iraq War legal advice to Cabinet colleagues. Another might have been a challenge to David Cameron's instruction that officials should not undertake contingency planning for a 'leave' vote in advance of the Brexit referendum.

The Constitution Society supported the proposal and suggested that a revised and extended version of the Cabinet Manual should be subject to Parliamentary approval.

This attempt to fetter Ministers' discretion was, of course no more welcome to the Government than had been the IfG's suggested Policy Directions (see above). Even so, the quality of the Government's two formal responses was disappointing.

Rather depressingly, since the proposal was clearly directed only at departures from established procedures, not the merits of a policy, the initial response completely misrepresented it as being "for a formal Ministerial direction to be given, if Ministers decided to go ahead with a policy against the advice of officials". Having set up this misrepresentation HMG then (quite rightly) rejected its own foolish proposal.

The second response wasn't much better. The rejection of the case for a procedural direction was based on a distinction between Accounting Officers' direct responsibility to Parliament and Permanent Secretaries' responsibility to Ministers and the Prime Minister for the conduct of departmental business. But this was a false distinction since Permanent Secretaries have a duty to Parliament as Accounting Officers for the efficient conduct of their departments.

The committee's first report, the Government's first response, the committee's second report and the Government's second response can all be read on the Understanding the Civil Service website[72].

6.5 Feasibility Directions

Feasibility Directions were introduced in 2011 and allowed officials to require Ministers to direct them to proceed with projects even if officials had put on record their doubts that the project's objectives could be achieved either at all, or within the timescale and resources stipulated by the Minister.

The Treasury defined feasibility as follows:

> Feasibility often overlaps with value for money and/or propriety. The judgement to be made is whether government has the ability to carry out the proposed policy effectively and credibly. Precedents, market testing and pilot studies can give confidence that a new policy or proposal will be feasible. Conversely, warning signs include novelty, high administration costs, high error rates and significant compliance costs. Where there is doubt about the quality of administration, the proposed course may well also be inefficient or improper.
>
> The deliverability assessment of a major project is also an aspect of feasibility. Where delivery concerns have been raised (for example, in a gateway review), the full accounting officer assessment would normally be expected to note those concerns, and reflect any mitigating actions taken or planned as a result. Although the accounting officer might expect to be notified of these concerns as soon as they are raised, it is preferable for the written assessment of feasibility to be prepared once any mitigating actions have been taken, so that the accounting officer to can also take those into account.

---

[72] https://www.civilservant.org.uk

Whitehall watchers awaited the first feasibility direction with great interest. Would it be seen as evidence, yet again, of Ministers unrealistic expectations, driven by short term political considerations? Or would it be evidence, yet again, of the need for Ministers to be able to override their cautious, unimaginative and unambitious civil servants?

It was quite telling, therefore, that a 2016 National Audit Office report asserted that Accounting Officers "appear to lack confidence to challenge Ministers where they have concerns about the feasibility or value for money of new policies or decisions, not least because standing up to Ministers is seen as damaging to a civil servant's career prospects".

Even then, nothing much appeared to change. *The Times* reported, in early 2019, that the retiring head of the National Audit Office , Sir Amyas Morse, was concerned that the balance of power between Ministers and senior civil servants had shifted, with officials increasingly unable to challenge bad decisions.

> "I still don't think we've sorted out the question of the interaction between the political agenda and delivering good results and value for money," Sir Amyas said. "There's pressure to do things too quickly or to announce very high-profile world-beating projects. Allowing Ministers to have a say in the appointment of senior officials has led to a position where Ministers have a great deal of power over their civil servants. That's unfortunate. They're intelligent people. They understand that the consequences of disagreeing with a Minister are likely to be pretty ugly."

The first Feasibility Direction eventually appeared in 2018 when a Minister took responsibility for the risks associated with accelerated introduction of new 'T Level' exams. This was a perfectly sensible and uncontentious use of the mechanism.

A small number of further Feasibility Directions were issued by the Business Secretary as his officials rushed to support the private sector during the 2020 Covid crisis.

6.6 Senior Responsible Officers

The 2013 introduction of SROs looked more promising. SROs were to be personally accountable, including to Parliament, for the delivery of major projects such as the National Cyber Security Programme. The key principle had until then been that civil servants who gave evidence to such committees do so "as the representative of the Minister in charge of the Department and subject to the Minister's instructions". But MPs could now, for the first time, question civil servants about their delivery of major projects such as the (delayed) introduction of Universal Credit. The new rules now provided that "Senior Responsible Owners (SROs) for Major Projects" are "expected to account for and explain the decisions and actions they have taken to deliver the projects for which they have personal responsibility".

It was hoped that newly appointed SROs might be concerned to ensure – before accepting their appointment – that they were not suffering from appraisal optimism, and that their project was properly resourced and had sensible times-cales and objectives. This would reduce the chances of their having to account to their Permanent Secretary and Parliament when things went wrong. And it would ensure that a senior official – the SRO – was forced to challenge Ministers if a major project were being established without proper resources etc. But it could work very badly if SROs were to do what officials had done in the past, which was to accept that Ministers are entitled to demand rapid action with limited resources, and so sign up to achieving what they privately believe to be unachievable.

In practice, little at first appeared to have changed. SRO appointment letters were little more than that. They specified neither the programme's objectives nor its resources or timescales. And most departments at first decided to appoint very senior staff as part-time SROs, rather than nominate those officials who were truly responsible for key projects. The SRO for the National Cyber Security Programme was for instance told that he would need to devote only two days a month to the role:-

> "I am writing ... to confirm your appointment as Senior Responsible Owner (SRO) of the National Cyber Security Programme ... This will be a part time role which requires two days per month. As SRO you have personal responsibility for delivery of National Cyber Security Programme and will be held accountable for the delivery of its objectives and policy intent; ..."

But SROs were strengthened by the introduction of Accounting Office Assessments - see further below. The (later stage) Universal Credit SRO appointment letter, for instance, required the SRO to prepare an Accounting Officer Assessment 'if the programme might depart from the four standards (regularity, propriety, value for money and feasibility), or from the agreed plan – including any contingency – in terms of costs, benefits, timescales, or level of risk'. It was also firmly linked to the Business Case, so the SRO was personally accountable for delivering the intended economic and net present values.

Indeed, the various publicly available Universal Credit appointment letters show that the relevant SRO was able to renegotiate the programmes timescales and be clear to Parliament what the reasons were. This will have followed private negotiations with his Ministers. So this particular Minister/official dynamic appeared to be working very well.

6.7 Accounting Officer Assessments

As from 2017, and following a Public Accounts Committee recommendation, the Treasury announced that '*Accounting Officers should personally approve, in advance, all significant initiatives, policies, programmes and projects*' and so be able to provide assurance to Parliament that those activities provide value for money and are feasible etc. The guidance went on to say (emphasis added):

> The analysis should consider the issue in the round. **A Ministerial policy decision cannot be sufficient justification alone for proceeding**. The accounting officer's job is to try to reconcile Ministers' policy objectives with the standards for use of public funds.

The full accounting officer assessment should provide a frank examination of the key issues including any sensitive issues. It should address the essence of the policy which is being delivered, its purposes and its prospect of successful delivery or implementation. It is therefore not usually published in full, but is shared with the Treasury. A summary of the key points from an accounting officer assessment of a major project should however be prepared and published.

Officials are not obliged to prepare an AO Assessment immediately a Minister indulges in some blue sky thinking. And the Treasury's guidance allows a bit of wriggle room later on:

> Often, big intricate decisions have long lead times. In such cases, it is good practice to make the accounting officer assessment in principle at an early point, firming it up at suitable strategic points as the policy or proposal is developed. This makes for orderly evaluation of the key features of the policy, with no surprises at the final decision point. Apart from providing time to redesign a policy or proposal, early assessment may flag up how the proposal can be better designed to meet both Ministers' and parliament's requirements, or whether there is a for a Ministerial (or board) direction, particularly when proposed spending is imminent or an existing spending stream no longer complies with the four accounting officer standards.

It is useful to distinguish *major projects* assessments from *policy* assessments.

The Treasury allows summaries of *major projects* assessments to be shared with MPs. Here is their guidance:

> Parliament has been given a role in monitoring 'major projects':

> Accounting officers who have considered an assessment for a project in the Government's Major Projects Portfolio (GMPP), in line with this guidance, and approved it, should provide to Parliament a summary of the key points from the assessment which informed their judgement.

But *policy* AO Assessments (for plans that fall outside the GMPP) do not need to be shared with Parliament. Here is the Treasury again:

> Accounting officers may choose to publish similar information from assessments made in other circumstances at their discretion, but there is no requirement to do so.

It is of course very unlikely that Accounting Officers will choose to publish the more controversial policy assessments. So MPs will not be able to assure themselves that sensible policy decisions are being made ... unless – perhaps supported by the National Audit Office and the media – Select Committees start insisting on seeing individual AO Assessments. If this were to happen, we might begin to see a significant improvement in the way this country is governed. But Parliament has seemed relatively weak since 2016, and possibly well before then, so this author, for one, is not optimistic.

My pessimism was not dissipated by an exchange in a Public Accounts Committee hearing in September 2020 when the PAC asked to see the Accounting Officer Assessment of the approach taken by Ministers in deciding which 'struggling' towns (and hence constituencies) were to benefit from the £3.6 billion *Towns Fund*. There were fears that too much politics had intruded into decision making but the relevant Permanent Secretary politely refused to publish his assessment of the program. "My understanding is that they are not normally published".

The Committee asked whether the Accounting Officer might nevertheless 'be willing for the Committee to have a private look at the papers? We have done this a number of times with other documents from Departments.' Next month, however, the Committee reported that (emphasis added):

> The £3.6 billion Towns Fund was introduced at pace by the Ministry of Housing, Communities and Local Government (the Department) in summer 2019. It relied upon Ministers selecting which towns would receive funding from a ranked list prepared by officials. The Department claims it had good reasons for this approach, but we are not convinced by the rationales for selecting some towns and not others. The justification offered by ministers for selecting individual towns are vague and based on sweeping assumptions. In some cases, towns were chosen by ministers despite being identified by officials as the very lowest priority (for example, one town selected ranked 535th out of 541 towns).
>
> **The Department has also not been open about the process it followed and it did not disclose the reasoning for selecting or excluding towns. This lack of transparency has fuelled accusations of political bias in the selection process, and has risked the Civil Service's reputation for integrity and impartiality. We are therefore disappointed that, although the Department's Permanent Secretary confirmed he was satisfied the selection process met the requirements of propriety and regularity, a summary of his Accounting Officer assessment remains unpublished.**
>
> It is still far from clear what impact the Department expects from the Towns Fund, when it expects to see the benefits, and how it will measure success both at the town level and across the whole programme. The Department says that it wished to give money to towns which it deemed unlikely to have the expertise to succeed at bidding for funding through an open competition; which also raises concerns about whether those

towns will have the capacity to spend the money well.

A July 2022 National Audit Office report about AO Assessments revealed that they could not tell how many AO assessments had been carried out. The NAO concluded that Accounting Officers were not consistently publishing and sharing their assessments in line with Treasury guidance. Many of the summaries that were published were published far too late to permit proper transparency and scrutiny. And those assessments that had been published did not always make clear that issues had been considered by AOs when making their judgements.

All in all, therefore, it does not appear that AO assessments are as yet achieving the objectives that were envisaged when they were introduced.

6.8 Will We Notice the Difference?

The story so far is that we don't have Policy or Procedural Directions but we do have Feasibility Directions, Senior Responsible Officers and Accounting Officer Assessments. Will they, after a slow start, eventually make a difference?

The author's view is that there will continue to be limited resistance from senior officials but the main problem is lack of interest from Parliament.

Civil Servants

Most senior officials would of course welcome improved policy- and other decision-making. But they worry that greater openness would in practice open up areas of conflict with their political masters and that would be new, scary territory.

Ex-Cabinet Secretary Sir Andrew Turnbull made this point when interviewed on the BBC's Westminster Hour in January 2015. Describing the 'bargain' entered into between Ministers and civil servants, he noted that the former benefit from frank advice and commitment from officials, but the civil servants are not then criticised publicly. If officials were to face public criticism then they would need a right of reply.

They would certainly appreciate the chance to push back when weaker ministers tell journalists that unpopular policy decisions were forced on them by their officials. It was, for instance, 'the Treasury' and 'civil servants who live in the South-East' who were apparently to blame for the decision not to extend HS2 to Leeds. This behaviour could not survive the introduction of true and honest accountability for civil servants.

Anonymity also suits senior civil servants, of course, when they do make mistakes. Many are understandably very reluctant to accept blame - especially as there are few comparable jobs outside the Senior Civil Service. Private sector execs who make mistakes can generally rebuild their careers elsewhere. Civil servants cannot.

The good news (as noted above) is that the introduction of SROs seems not to have damaged any individual minister-official relationships. The Universal Credit SRO was able to develop a positive relationship with their minister during the later stages of Universal Credit implementation - and the result appears to have been the exceptional response to the pressures that the Universal Credit system faced during the Covid pandemic. It is to be hoped that other SRO/ministerial teams will be similarly successful.

Much the same applies to Feasibility Directions and AO Assessments. Previous types of Ministerial Direction were once regarded as nuclear weapons - more effective in the silo rather than launched. But they have come to be seen as a grown-up way of allowing Ministers to account for political decisions to override strict value for money criteria. SROs' ability to prepare Accounting Officer Assessments are similarly unlikely to be used every day, but they might, over time, help curb Ministers' desire to order officials to achieve challenging objectives within impossible timescales and with inadequate resources.

MPs

Accountability is effective only if those being held to account know that their behaviour will be judged in a fair and consistent way against a clear model. If they will not be judged in this way then they will not adjust their behaviour to meet the needs of that model.

It follows that if civil servants are to become more publicly accountable then their those who judge them need to have clear principles which are consistent with the Civil Service Code. Can MPs be trusted to be good judges? The signs are not good.

House of Commons Select Committees are supposed to investigate the causes of both policy successes and policy failures with a view to learning lessons rather than ascribing blame. They typically call for a wide range of evidence including from experts outside government, and they often analyse issues very thoroughly. But their influence is severely curtailed by ministers' insistence that civil servants who appear before such committees (other than the Public Accounts Committee) do so under instruction from Ministers[73]. Officials giving evidence are accordingly cautious and defensive, and these traits are carried through - with perhaps more serious consequences - when drafting departmental evidence and responses to committee reports.

Select Committees can also often appear to be more interested in seeking political advantage than in learning useful lessons. MPs will often question in unfair or unreasonable ways in order to make political points and/or to appear 'strong' in the eyes of their colleagues and constituents. They also sometimes criticise officials when they cannot get at responsible Ministers, or at other responsible civil servants. Such behaviour certainly catches the attention of Whitehall - and sometimes the media. The resultant video may get plenty of 'views', especially on social media. But civil service colleagues rally behind such victims so that this form of 'accountability' leads neither to career detriment nor to any change in the behaviour of the victims or others.

Even the Public Accounts Committee (the PAC) seldom

---

[73] See Part 1.4 - The Osmotherly Rules

attempts to exert real influence over the way the government machine is managed. Most Accounting Officers' primary aim, when dealing with the NAO or the PAC, is to avoid censure. They appear to assume that they won't learn anything from such interactions, and they don't believe that the purpose of the exercise is to improve or learn in any way. Worse still, many very good PAC reports have little or no impact. There is no follow up. The reports seldom if ever feature in civil service training programmes – although videos of embarrassed Accounting Officers certainly do, thus encouraging further defensiveness. Apart from this, everyone involved in a report just shrugs and moves on to the next issue.

Michael Coolican reinforces this impression in his book *No Tradesmen and No Women*:

> The repetitive nature of the issues that come before the Public Accounts Committee reinforces the point that there is little interest amongst civil servants in learning from the mistakes of others. Although more senior civil servants are aware of the committee, its reports are not widely read and so it is not surprising that the lessons are not absorbed.

Why do MPs show such little interest in holding the executive to account?

Their behaviour can in part be explained by their character and experience. Politicians are tribal animals and the vast majority have little or no interest in, or experience of, managing large organisations, or even in policy-making. Their career prospects depend upon their debating and deal-making skills and upon their ability to attract favourable media attention, not on their effectiveness in Select Committees.

Most of the media, too, have little interest in government itself, as distinct from its personalities. As Robert Saunders ruefully commented following the First Reading of the Safety of Rwanda Bill in December 2023:

> So much of the news coverage of the Rwanda vote is about what it means for the PM's authority, rather than its implications for policy, for the constitution &, indeed, for asylum-seekers. Respectfully, if that's all we're going to focus on, it might as well be in the sports news.

Politicians therefore focus on gaining political advantage by criticising fellow politicians, and Ministers in particular, rather than unelected officials. It can be fun to tear into hapless officials, but there are no votes in it.

Ministers, for their part, are reluctant to admit that they are not solely responsible for important decisions and achievements. Every senior official is well used to ministers claiming full public credit for a successful negotiation or initiative to which they have devoted only a tiny fraction of the time devoted by their officials. (To be fair, however, most decent ministers are very grateful in private.)

Ministers who appear to have made poor decisions will not want to publish the advice they receive. They would of course be happy to do so if the advice had proved to be poor, for they might then be excused for following it. But they wouldn't want to publish advice which was correct - and which they had ignored. As they could hardly be allowed to pick and choose which advice to publish, they can't or won't publish anything, and so blame cannot be allocated or shared.

MPs also want to be able to continue to write to fellow MPs (currently serving as ministers) about all aspects of a department's performance. Their constituents are much more impressed by 'a letter to the Minister' than by a letter to an official, even though they usually amount to the same thing. A small number of MPs have even refused to correspond with Agency Chief Executives, for instance about Driver and Vehicle Licensing decisions.

All in all, therefore, both I and many other commentators think it highly unlikely that either Parliament or the media will begin to hold government to account any time soon. David Allen Green nicely summarised the position in a January 2024 Substack:

> Few if any sensible people expect our current political system to require ministers to be honest. Reply-guys and other cynics may aver that it was ever thus: but the resignation of John Profumo seems not only long ago but in another political universe.
>
> This wide acceptance of political dishonesty does not remove the demand, at times, for our ministers to be honest. And it also does not remove the demand, at times, for ministers to provide true and full information. What it means is that the demand for accountability has switched from parliament and our media to judicial and quasi-judicial processes, such as judicial reviews and public inquests.
>
> In judicial and quasi-judicial processes, ministers and senior officials give evidence under pain of the criminal offence of perjury. They are also obliged to disclose information under the potential (and sometimes actual) pain of court orders. They may hold the public in contempt, and they may also be in contempt of parliament; but contempt of court is

still a thing that matters.

Perhaps this is why certain types of politician and pundit want to discredit and remove any judicial and quasi-judicial accountability for those with public power. Perhaps.

But, to take two examples familiar to readers of this Substack: it should not have been the Supreme Court that exposed that no minister or official would sign a statement of truth as the genuine reasons for the infamous 2019 prorogation; and it should not have been the Covid inquiry that compelled ministers and former ministers and advisers to disclose the true substance of what was going on (and not going on) during the pandemic.

In both cases it really should have been parliament and/or the news media forcing this hard accountability against an unwilling executive. But it was left to statutory powers of disclosure and the formal requirements for witness evidence instead.

Some may complain that this meant there are judges and lawyers over-stepping some mark. But the sad reality is that it has ended up with judicial and quasi-judicial processes because the political processes have failed to get to the hearts of the matters. The problem is not so much judicial and legalistic expansionism, but a collapse of political accountability by any other form.

This is not a good thing. The solution, however, is not to attack those remaining aspects of our polity that can force accountability on reluctant office holders and officials, but to make parliamentary and other forms of democratic accountability stronger.

It should not take a judicial review or a public inquiry to properly hold a minister or official to account; yet if that is all we have got then, it there is no alternative.

Chapter 7
End Notes

Chapters 1 to 3 of this book include a description of civil servants' duties and responsibilities as they were first summarised in my book How to be a Civil Servant. That text was cleared, in advance of publication in 2000 and again in 2004, by the Cabinet Office, where I once worked. I am not aware that the Cabinet Office has subsequently announced any significant changes to those duties and responsibilities.

I have added a considerable amount of further material and comment, drawing as far as possible on official publications as well as on think tank, academic and other expert writing. This principally appears in Chapter 1.2.3 (The Haldane

Report), Chapter 2.2.8 (Compliance with the Law) and Chapters 4 to 6. To the best of my knowledge, the resultant text is accurate as of January 2024.

My personal style guide mandates Minister (not minister) and civil servant/service (rather than Civil Servant/Service) except where quoting document titles or other writers.

I would be very grateful if readers would draw my attention to any errors or omissions. Notifications of stray or missing apostrophes, and similar gaffes, are of course also welcome. My email address for this purpose is ukcs68@gmail.com. Any necessary changes to the text will then be listed on the Understanding the Civil Service website and incorporated in future editions.

Please also do not hesitate to suggest ways in which the text might be clarified or improved. And, if you have found this book helpful, please recommend it to others and/or add Amazon reviews. These will encourage me to produce further editions for other readers.

__Martin Stanley__

London

January 2024